DIGITAL MARKETING

LEARN DIGITAL MARKETING THE SMART AND SIMPLE WAY

Dr Richa Agarwal
Chandan Gupta

First published in 2026 by Hachette India
(Registered name: Hachette Book Publishing India Pvt. Ltd)
www.hachetteindia.com

1

ISBN 978-93-5731-701-6

Hachette Book Publishing India Pvt. Ltd
4th & 5th Floors, Corporate Centre
Plot No. 94, Sector 44, Gurugram – 122003, India

Typeset in Adobe Garamond Pro 11.5/16
by Content Respondus
New Delhi

Printed and bound in India
by Manipal Technologies Limited

DIGITAL MARKETING

LEARN DIGITAL MARKETING THE SMART AND SIMPLE WAY

Dr Richa Agarwal is an academic and independent researcher with a PhD in Commerce, currently serving as an assistant professor. Her teaching and research interests span commerce, management, and the evolving domain of digital marketing, where she explores the integration of traditional business concepts with contemporary digital practices.

Dr Agarwal is also a reviewer for various reputed academic journals, contributing to the advancement of research standards and scholarly work. She is committed to fostering analytical thinking, research excellence, and practical learning among students.

Chandan Gupta is a digital marketing expert with over eleven years of experience in performance marketing, lead generation, and online brand growth. He has worked across multiple industries, helping organizations build strong digital strategies and achieve measurable results. Chandan is passionate about sharing practical marketing knowledge and empowering learners through training and content creation.

Contents

Image Credits

Page 15: Vlada Karpovich/Pexels
Page 32: Miriam Alonso/Pexels
Page 105: Andrea Piacquadio/Pexels
Page 150: Pixabay
Infographics are created by Content Respondus (©Hachette India)
Pages 72, 100, 102, 103, 105, 120, 164, 167: Screenshots used are provided by the authors

Note from the Authors

We wrote this book with one goal in mind: to make digital marketing simple, practical, and accessible for beginners. Whether you are a student, entrepreneur, freelancer, or business owner, digital marketing gives you the power to grow your ideas and reach audiences far beyond your local boundaries.

You don't need to master every tool or platform at once. Begin with what feels comfortable, experiment regularly, track your results, and learn from them. Consistency and curiosity will take you further than perfection.

The internet is an ever-changing world of possibilities. Each update, algorithm, and innovation opens new doors for creativity and connection. Stay curious, keep learning, and use these tools responsibly and ethically to make a positive impact.

We hope this book will help you gain clarity, confidence, and inspiration to take your first meaningful steps into the digital world.

Chapter 1

Introduction to Digital Marketing

What is Digital Marketing?

Digital marketing refers to the practice of promoting products, services, or brands through digital channels such as the internet and electronic devices. It is often referred to as online marketing or internet marketing as it primarily involves platforms like websites, search engines, social media, mobile apps, email, and even SMS.

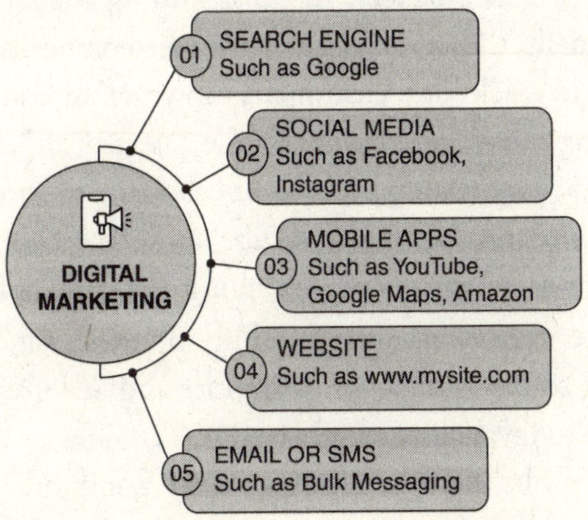

Fig. 1.1: Digital marketing platforms

In today's world, people spend a significant amount of time on their smartphones, tablets, or computers, scrolling through social media, watching YouTube videos, searching for information on Google or shopping online. According to a Statista (2024) report, the average global user spends over six hours a day online, making digital channels the most effective way for businesses to connect with their audiences.

Unlike traditional marketing methods, such as newspapers, radio, or television advertisements, digital marketing is more interactive, measurable, and cost-effective. It allows businesses to engage directly with their target audience, track user behaviour, and customize their campaigns in real time, using analytics tools like Google Analytics or Google Search Console.

Let's See How It Works: A Practical Example

Imagine a small bakery that has just opened in a city. Traditionally, the owner might have relied on newspaper ads or flyers to reach local customers. However, by using digital marketing, the bakery owner now creates an Instagram page to post appealing pictures of cakes and pastries, shares short baking tutorials on YouTube, and runs a Google Ads campaign to target people searching for phrases like 'best chocolate cake near me'. In addition, the business sends discount coupons through its website and SMS/WhatsApp database to loyal customers.

This multi-platform strategy that combines content, search, and direct marketing is an example of integrated digital marketing, which not only boosts brand awareness but also drives customer engagement and sales conversion more efficiently (Ryan 2020). Such strategies are particularly effective for small and medium enterprises (SMEs) due to their low cost and high impact.

Fig. 1.2: Traditional and digital marketing offerings

Traditional vs Digital Marketing

Marketing has always played a vital role in helping businesses connect with their customers. It involves informing people about a product or service and persuading them to act, often through a purchase or inquiry. Over time, the way businesses communicate with their target audience has evolved significantly due to technological advancements and changes in consumer behaviour.

In earlier decades, companies primarily relied on traditional marketing methods to promote their offerings. These included tools such as newspaper advertisements, radio announcements, TV commercials, billboards, magazines, and pamphlets. These channels were effective in reaching large groups of people at once. For example, a commercial aired during a popular television show could be viewed by millions of households while a full-page newspaper ad could deliver the brand message to thousands of readers in a single day (Belch & Belch 2018).

Traditional marketing, although still relevant in some sectors, is generally less interactive, harder to measure, and more expensive. Campaigns often require significant investments in printing, media buying, and production and offer limited targeting capabilities. The same message is broadcast to a broad audience regardless of their interest or buying behaviour.

A Clear Shift in Trend

The way businesses approach marketing has changed dramatically, particularly with the rise of the internet, smartphones, and social media. According to the Digital 2024 Report by DataReportal, over 5.3 billion people worldwide now use the internet, creating a massive shift in how brands reach and interact with their audiences.

Digital marketing emerged as a solution that is more affordable, targeted, data-driven, and interactive. Unlike traditional media, digital platforms allow businesses to reach specific audiences based on factors like age, location, interests, and online behaviour. It also enables two-way communication, allowing brands to receive immediate feedback and adjust campaigns in real time.

Furthermore, digital marketing makes it easier to track performance, using tools like Google Analytics, Google

Webmaster, or Google Tag Manager, which provide data on website traffic, conversions, user behaviour, and more. This level of insight is rarely possible in traditional marketing, where measuring reach and impact is often based on estimates (Tiago & Veríssimo 2014).

Limitations of Traditional Marketing

Traditional marketing includes methods like newspaper ads, radio spots, TV commercials, billboards, brochures, posters, and flyers. While these methods were once the backbone of business promotion, they now face several limitations:

- **High cost:** Traditional marketing is often expensive. Businesses must pay for printing, media space, production, distribution, and labour. For example, airing a TV commercial or printing a full-page newspaper ad can cost lakhs of rupees, making it difficult to afford for small businesses.
- **Limited reach:** Most traditional campaigns are local or regional. A newspaper ad may only reach readers in one city, and a billboard only targets people who pass that location. Expanding reach to other areas involves additional expenses.
- **No targeting:** Traditional marketing casts a wide net. The same message is shown to everyone, regardless of their interest, age, or background. For example, a billboard promoting baby products will be seen by all age groups, even those who are not potential buyers.
- **Difficult to track results:** One of the biggest drawbacks is the lack of data. It's hard to tell how many people saw

the advertisement, how they responded, or whether it led to a sale. This makes it difficult for businesses to measure success or improve future campaigns.

The Rise of Digital Marketing

With the rapid growth of internet access and mobile usage, especially following the COVID-19 pandemic, digital marketing has emerged as a smarter, faster, and more affordable way to reach customers (McKinsey & Company 2020).

According to the Digital 2024 Global Overview Report by DataReportal (in partnership with We Are Social and Meltwater), over 535 crore (5.35 billion) people, which is 66.2 per cent of the global population, were using the internet as of January 2024. This dramatic rise in internet penetration has shifted the focus of marketing from traditional channels to digital platforms, allowing businesses to engage instantly, globally, and more cost-effectively than ever before.

Unlike traditional advertising methods that often rely on physical materials and costly media placements, digital marketing allows businesses to connect with their audience in real time through various online platforms.

Some of the most used digital marketing platforms include the following:

- Google (search and display ads)
- Facebook and Instagram (social media marketing)
- YouTube (video marketing)
- Websites and blogs (content marketing)
- Email and SMS (direct marketing)
- Mobile apps (app-based engagement)

Traditional vs Digital Marketing in Action: The Journey of Bunaai (Jaipur)

Let's see how it works. An emphatic example of the shift from traditional to digital marketing can be seen in the story of Bunaai, an ethnic boutique brand founded in Jaipur. In its early days, the brand relied mainly on traditional promotional methods such as printing brochures, advertising in local fashion magazines, and participating in city exhibitions. Although these methods brought some initial walk-in traffic, there was no accurate way to know how many people saw the ads or whether the promotions directly resulted in sales. Moreover, printing new materials for every festive season or fashion launch increased marketing expenses.

After the COVID-19 pandemic, consumer buying habits shifted dramatically towards social media and online shopping (McKinsey & Company 2020). Responding to this trend, Bunaai began posting styling videos and product catalogues on Instagram and Facebook, collaborating with micro-influencers, sharing behind-the-scenes reels, and running targeted social media ads for women aged between twenty and thirty-five across major Indian cities. The brand also introduced a direct WhatsApp ordering option, making the customer journey easier and faster.

The Results?

- Within a few days, the page gained hundreds of followers.
- Customers started placing online orders and visiting the shop after seeing posts.

- The store could track user engagement, such as how many people saw, liked, shared, or clicked the ad.
- Bunaai saved money compared to printing and distributing physical pamphlets.
- The store owner was able to interact with customers directly through messages and comments.

This transition from traditional to digital marketing not only reduced costs but also increased visibility, engagement, and sales. Today Bunaai continues to rely on digital platforms as a core part of its marketing strategy.

Real-World Brand Comparisons

This shift is not limited to small businesses. Many well-known Indian brands also show the contrast between digital-first and traditional marketing approaches. Here are a few of them:

- **Amul**®, once famous for billboards, print ads, and its iconic 'Amul Girl' campaign, now maintains a strong presence on social media platforms such as Instagram, Facebook, and YouTube. The brand continues to grow, with revenue reaching approximately ₹90,000 crore (about $90 billion) in FY 2024–25. This indicates that digital engagement has helped Amul remain relevant even decades after its traditional advertising success. (Economic Times 2023).
- **Nykaa**®, a digital-native beauty brand, built its entire business model through social media campaigns, influencer partnerships, and performance marketing,

without relying on conventional print or TV advertising in its early years (Business Standard 2022).

- boAt®, a home-grown audio and wearables brand, has built its success primarily through digital channels such as social media, influencer collaborations, e-commerce platforms, and online advertising. This digital-first strategy enabled the brand to scale rapidly across India and compete directly with global brands in an online-driven market. (KPMG 2021).

These examples highlight how businesses of all sizes are increasingly prioritizing digital marketing tools to reach the right audience, improve brand loyalty, and measure success in real time.

Adapting to Change: Lessons from the COVID-19 Pandemic

The shift to digital marketing became even more crucial during the COVID-19 pandemic, when many traditional businesses moved online to survive. Local *kirana* stores started taking orders via WhatsApp, and large companies launched Instagram and Facebook campaigns to reach customers remotely. Even the education sector, which previously relied heavily on printed books, pivoted to online learning, apps, and digital content for schools, students, and teachers.

These changes proved that digital marketing is not just an option; it is a lifeline for business continuity and long-term growth strategy.

Types of Digital Marketing Channels (Overview)

Digital marketing includes a broad set of online strategies that help businesses promote their products or services, reach the right audience, and achieve measurable marketing goals. Each channel serves a distinct purpose, and successful marketers often integrate several methods to build a strong and dynamic digital presence (Chaffey & Ellis-Chadwick 2019).

1. **Search engine optimization (SEO):** SEO is the process of enhancing a website's content, structure, and technical performance to achieve higher rankings in unpaid (organic) search results on platforms like Google and Bing search engines. This approach improves visibility and drives traffic by aligning content with user search intent. It is one of the most cost-effective long-term marketing strategies.
2. **Search engine marketing (SEM):** SEM involves paid advertisements that appear on search engine result pages (SERPs). Tools like Google Ads allow businesses to bid on keywords so their ads appear above organic results. This method, commonly referred to as pay-per-click (PPC), only charges businesses when someone clicks the ad, making it highly performance-based and ideal for immediate visibility.
3. **Paid marketing (performance marketing):** Performance marketing includes paid campaigns across platforms like Google, Facebook, Instagram, and YouTube, where advertisers only pay when specific actions occur (e.g., clicks, video views, or conversions). Marketers use this

model to target users based on age, location, interests, behaviours, or look-alike audience. It delivers faster, more measurable results and is ideal for product launches, lead generation, branding and promotions (Chaffey & Smith 2022).

4. **Social media marketing (SMM):** SMM involves using platforms like Facebook, Instagram, X, LinkedIn, and YouTube to share content, engage with followers and promote brands. It is a powerful tool for community building, customer service, and brand awareness and supports both organic and paid promotional strategies.
5. **Content marketing:** Content marketing focuses on creating and sharing valuable content such as blogs, articles, infographics, videos, and guides to educate, inform, or entertain a target audience. Rather than direct selling, it builds trust and authority over time (Pulizzi 2014).
6. **Influencer marketing:** Influencer marketing involves collaborations with individuals who have a loyal digital following. These influencers promote products in a personal and relatable way, often influencing purchase decisions through authentic recommendations.
7. **Affiliate marketing:** In affiliate marketing, third parties, such as bloggers, YouTubers, or influencers, earn a commission for driving traffic or sales to a business using special referral links. It's low-risk and cost-effective as brands pay only for measurable results (Patel 2022).
8. **Email and SMS marketing:** This method involves sending personalized emails or SMS messages to customers to promote offers, send newsletters, or nurture relationships.

Despite the rise of newer platforms, it remains effective for customer retention and re-engagement, particularly in sectors like retail and education.

9. **Video marketing:** Video marketing uses short- and long-form video content to attract and engage audiences. Platforms like YouTube Shorts, Instagram Reels, and Facebook Shorts are widely used to share tutorials, testimonials, product demos, and more. Video is among the most engaging content formats, driving high recall and conversion rates (Wyzowl 2024).
10. **Web analytics and CRM tools:** While not direct channels, tools like Google Analytics, GTM (Google Tag Manager) and customer relationship management (CRM) are critical in digital marketing. They help measure campaign effectiveness, track user behaviour, and manage customer relationships. These tools allow marketers to make data-driven decisions, optimize strategies, and improve overall return on investment.

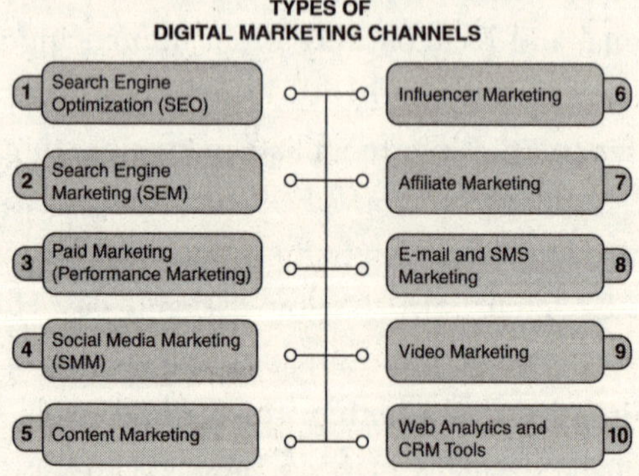

Fig. 1.3: Types of digital marketing

Each digital marketing channel has its own unique strengths and advantages. Successful marketers often use a combination of channels based on their specific business requirements, budget and target audience. Understanding how these channels work and how they can work together is the first step towards building a strong, effective digital marketing strategy.

Career Scope and Growth in Digital Marketing

Digital marketing is no longer just a way to promote products and services. It has grown into a high-demand, skill-based career path that appeals to students, freshers, freelancers, entrepreneurs, and experienced professionals alike. As more businesses go online, the demand for skilled digital marketers has increased significantly across sectors such as e-commerce, education, healthcare, hospitality, real estate and retail.

According to LinkedIn's Jobs, job titles like digital marketing specialist, SEO analyst, and performance marketing manager are among the fastest-growing roles in India. This shift reflects the broader digital transformation that accelerated during and after the COVID-19 pandemic, as businesses turned to online platforms in order to maintain operations.

These are some of the most popular roles in this field:

- Social media manager
- SEO executive
- Google Ads (PPC – pay-per-click) specialist
- Content writer or content marketer

- Email marketing executive
- Influencer marketing executive
- Affiliate marketing manager

With experience and continuous learning, professionals can grow into senior positions, such as digital marketing strategist and digital marketing consultant, or even start their own freelance business or digital marketing agency. Certification programmes from platforms like Google, LinkedIn Learning, HubSpot, Coursera, Udemy, and local universities help learners build practical skills and improve their job prospects.

Work Opportunities and Global Exposure

While flexibility exists in many professions today, digital marketing offers a wider range of work formats because the entire workflow is digital. Campaign planning, content creation, SEO, analytics, and performance ads can all be executed online, which allows professionals to work with clients and companies across cities and countries without physical presence. As a result, digital marketers commonly find opportunities in full-time roles as well as freelancing and project-based contracts, both in India and globally. A Statista survey (2024) reported that more than 40 per cent of digital marketing professionals in India work remotely or in hybrid roles, especially in content creation, SEO, PPC, and social media management. This shift has made the profession highly attractive to those looking for location-independent careers, such as freelancers, digital nomads, and solopreneurs.

Fig. 1.4: Work flexibility for freelance work

Additionally, the rise of freelance platforms like Upwork, Fiverr and Freelancer.com has made it easier for skilled marketers to connect with international clients and earn in foreign currencies. This global access is a major reason why digital marketing is often considered a borderless career.

Opportunities for Entrepreneurs and Small Businesses

Digital marketing has proven to be a game-changer for entrepreneurs and small business owners, offering them cost-effective tools to grow their business and compete with larger players. Unlike traditional methods, such as print advertisements, radio jingles, or hoardings, which require high budgets and offer limited targeting, digital marketing enables precise outreach at a fraction of the cost (Meta for Business 2023).

Even a local shop or service provider can now

- promote products or services on Facebook, Instagram, or WhatsApp Business,
- run affordable geo-targeted ads to reach nearby customers,
- set up a basic e-commerce store or accept orders via chat platforms,
- expand beyond local boundaries using social media, Google Search, and content marketing,
- build a personal brand by consistently sharing helpful or engaging content.

These strategies empower businesses to scale up without needing a large marketing team or budget. According to the McKinsey Global SME Digital Survey (2021), digitally active small businesses grow revenues up to twice as fast as those using only traditional channels.

Furthermore, Meta India's Small Business Report (2023) highlighted that 91 per cent of surveyed SMEs found social media marketing essential for survival and growth, especially during and after the COVID-19 pandemic.

By using digital tools effectively, entrepreneurs can take full control of their business narrative, develop loyal customer communities, and achieve scalable growth with low initial investment.

Quick Bytes

- Digital marketing means using the internet and digital platforms to promote products or services.
- It is more affordable, better targeted, and easier to measure than traditional marketing.

- Traditional methods like newspapers, TV, and hoardings are expensive, less focused, and hard to track.
- Digital marketing offers good career options in areas like SEO, content writing, and online advertising.
- Small businesses and entrepreneurs can grow online using digital tools at a lower cost.
- Learning digital marketing is important for career growth, freelancing, and business success in today's online world.

Self-Assessment Questions *(For Revision and Reflection)*

1. What makes digital marketing more effective than traditional marketing in today's world?
2. How does the example of Bunaai show the shift from traditional to digital marketing?
3. List any five major digital marketing channels discussed in the chapter and explain their purpose in brief.
4. Why is digital marketing considered a strong career option today?
5. How does digital marketing support entrepreneurs and small businesses more than traditional marketing?

References

1. George E. Belch and Michael A. Belch, *Advertising and Promotion: An Integrated Marketing Communications Perspective*, 11th ed. (New York: McGraw-Hill Education, 2018).

2. 'How Nykaa Built a Digital Beauty Empire', *Business Standard*, 2022.
3. Dave Chaffey and Fiona Ellis-Chadwick, *Digital Marketing*, 7th ed. (Harlow, UK: Pearson Education, 2019).
4. Dave Chaffey and P. R. Smith, *Digital Marketing Excellence*, 6th ed. (London: Routledge, 2022).
5. DataReportal, *Digital 2024: Global Overview Report* (We Are Social and Meltwater, 2024).
6. *Economic Times*, 'How Amul Is Staying Relevant in the Digital Age', 2023.
7. KPMG, *Digital-First Brands and the Evolution of Marketing in India* (2021).
8. McKinsey & Company, *The COVID-19 Recovery Will Be Digital: A Plan for the First 90 Days* (2020).
9. McKinsey & Company, *The Rise of Digital SMEs in India* (2021).
10. Meta for Business, *Empowering Small Businesses in India* (2023).
11. Neil Patel, *Affiliate Marketing Made Simple* (2022).
12. Joe Pulizzi, *Epic Content Marketing* (New York: McGraw-Hill Education, 2014).
13. Damian Ryan, *Understanding Digital Marketing: Marketing Strategies for Engaging the Digital Generation* (London: Kogan Page, 2020).
14. Statista, *Average Daily Time Spent Online Worldwide* (2024).
15. Statista, *Global Digital Population as of January 2024* (2024).

16. Statista, *Global Freelance Platform Usage Statistics* (2024).
17. Statista, *Remote Work in Digital Marketing: India Report* (2024).
18. Maria Teresa Tiago and José Manuel Veríssimo, 'Digital Marketing and Social Media: Why Bother?' *Business Horizons* 57, no. 6 (2014): 703–708.
19. Wyzowl, *State of Video Marketing Report 2024* (2024).

Chapter 2

Understanding the Digital Consumer

Digital Buying Behaviour

Digital buying behaviour refers to how people use the internet to search for, compare, and purchase products or services. The increasing use of smartphones, social media, and shopping apps has changed the way that people shop. Today's customers are more informed, connected, and quick to make decisions.

Earlier, people used to go to physical stores, talk to salespeople, and buy products directly. But now most shopping journeys begin online. Customers do not just look at the product; they also read reviews, compare prices, check delivery options, and follow the brand on social media before deciding.

Here is a simple view of a typical digital buying journey:

- **Search:** The customer begins by searching for products on Google or asking for suggestions on social media platforms.
- **Compare:** They explore various websites or apps, read reviews, and compare features and pricing.

- **Engage:** To build trust, they may follow the brand on social media, watch videos, or read frequently asked questions (FAQs) and testimonials.

Fig. 2.1: Buyer behaviour process

- **Decide:** Once confident, they make a purchase through a website, mobile app, or even via chat platforms like WhatsApp.
- **Share Feedback:** After the purchase, they often leave reviews or share their experiences online, impacting future buyers.

This process is known as the digital customer journey, and it is often completed using smartphones. As modern buyers are more informed and selective, businesses need to pay attention not only to what they offer but also to how they present their brand online. A strong digital presence, supported by clear product information, quick responses, and reliable customer service, plays a vital role in attracting and retaining customers (Kotler et al. 2021). By understanding digital buying behaviour, marketers can design more effective strategies, convert interest into sales, and build lasting customer relationships.

Why is Digital Buying Behaviour Important for Marketers?

Understanding digital buying behaviour is essential for marketers because it allows them to connect with customers in meaningful and effective ways. In today's highly competitive market, simply promoting a product is not enough. Marketers must understand what customers are looking for, where they search for information, how they compare different options, and what factors influence their final decisions. This insight enables businesses to deliver more personalized and impactful marketing strategies.

Below are several reasons why knowing digital buying behaviour is valuable for marketers:

- **Helps create relevant content:** When marketers understand common customer questions and concerns, they can create useful content, such as FAQs, product comparisons, buying guides, and explainer videos. This type of content not only educates potential buyers but also builds trust by addressing their doubts early in the buying journey.
- **Improves ad targeting:** Digital buying behaviour provides insights into customer demographics, preferences, and online habits. Marketers can use this data to create well-targeted advertisements. For example, if women aged 20–35 are searching for fashion accessories, marketers can run visually appealing ads on platforms like Instagram or Pinterest, where this audience is more active.
- **Builds brand trust:** Modern consumers rely heavily on social proof, such as customer reviews, ratings, testimonials, and influencer recommendations, before making a purchase. By promoting genuine user experiences and encouraging customer feedback, marketers can build credibility and increase confidence in the brand.

- **Enhances the user experience:** A smooth and engaging user experience is critical to converting visitors into customers. If a website is slow to load, hard to navigate, or lacks customer support, potential buyers are likely to leave. By understanding what customers expect, marketers can improve website design, provide quick-loading pages, offer live chat or chatbot support, and ensure that helpful information is easy to find.
- **Increases conversions and customer loyalty:** When the online buying process is simple, personalized and satisfying, it encourages more visitors to make purchases. Satisfied customers are more likely to return and recommend the brand to others, which leads to long-term loyalty and business growth.

The Customer Journey (Awareness to Conversion)

The customer journey refers to the entire process a person goes through from first learning about a product or service to finally purchasing it and continuing to interact with the brand afterwards. In the digital age, this journey often happens quickly and across multiple online platforms, such as social media, search engines, and e-commerce websites. It is also more trackable and measurable compared to traditional methods, allowing marketers to analyse customer behaviour in real time.

The digital customer journey is divided into five key stages:

1. **Awareness:** This is the first stage, where a potential customer becomes aware of a brand, product, or service. At this point, the person may not yet have an immediate

need, but exposure to marketing content catches their attention. Visibility is crucial at this stage because many consumers do not start with intent. Instead, they are influenced by what they see online. Therefore, creative and engaging content can plant the seed for interest (Edelman and Singer 2015).

- **Goal:** Increase visibility and make the target audience aware of your offering.
- **Tools:** Social media posts, blog articles, influencer mentions, YouTube ads and Google display ads.

Example: A person may struggle with low tyre pressure but never thinks about buying a portable car inflator. When they see an Instagram video showing how easy to use it is, they suddenly realize they need it. Their demand existed, but it was hidden, or 'latent'.

> In marketing, **consumer demand** is usually categorized into two key types: effective demand and latent demand. **Effective demand** refers to situations where consumers already recognize a need and are actively looking for a solution. For example, someone experiencing frequent tyre punctures will deliberately search for a reliable tyre inflator. In contrast, **latent demand** refers to a need that exists but is not yet recognized by the consumer until they are exposed to a solution. Digital marketing plays a major role in both types of demand. It helps capture effective demand through tools like search ads, SEO and comparison content, while at the same time unlocking latent demand through engaging visual content, influencer marketing and social media storytelling that introduce new solutions.

2. **Interest:** Once someone is aware of the product, they may become curious and begin exploring more details. This is the stage where they start seeking information to understand how the product works and whether it fits their needs. At this stage, marketers need to create content that educates and engages while building trust.
   - **Goal:** Provide clear, engaging and helpful information.
   - **Tools:** Product demos, tutorials, explainer blogs, social media pages and comparison articles.

   Example: The user watches a how-to-use video on YouTube or scrolls through your Instagram page for more information.
3. **Consideration:** Here the customer is actively evaluating options. They compare brands, read reviews, check features, and assess whether the product solves their problem or adds value. Even small details like positive reviews or transparent policies can strongly influence a customer's decision.
   - **Goal:** Build trust and offer reasons to choose your product.
   - **Tools:** Customer reviews, product comparison charts, pricing details, return policies, FAQs, and retargeting ads.

     Example: They compare your product with others on Amazon, read reviews, and explore discount offers or flexible returns.
4. **Conversion (Purchase):** This is the action phase, where the customer decides to buy. The focus here is to make the transaction as smooth and convenient as possible.

According to the Baymard Institute (2023), a confusing or slow checkout process can lead to cart abandonment. Therefore, providing a seamless purchasing experience is essential for boosting conversion rates.

- **Goal:** Reduce friction in the buying process.
- **Tools:** Easy checkout systems, secure payment methods, clear call-to-action buttons, and WhatsApp ordering for small businesses.

Example: The customer adds the item to their cart, completes payment, or places an order via WhatsApp.

5. **Post-Purchase (Loyalty and Advocacy):** The journey does not end with a purchase. After-sales engagement is important for building loyalty and turning customers into brand advocates.
   - **Goal:** Encourage repeat purchases and word-of-mouth promotion.
   - **Tools:** Thank-you emails, discount codes, loyalty programmes, referral rewards, customer support, and review requests.

   Example: The customer receives a thank-you message and a discount for their next order and is encouraged to share their experience on social media. A positive post-purchase experience increases the likelihood of customer retention and referrals, which reduces future marketing costs.

Why Are These Stages Important?

In digital marketing, success is not just about making a sale; it is about guiding the customer smoothly through every step of the journey, from initial awareness to post-purchase backing. Understanding each stage of the customer journey allows marketers to engage more effectively with their audience. It helps them

- deliver the right message at the right time,
- select the most suitable platform for communication,
- develop content that matches the customer's needs at each stage,
- reduce marketing costs through more accurate targeting,
- increase conversion rates and build long-term customer loyalty.

Challenges in Influencing the Digital Customer Journey

Among the five stages of the digital customer journey, the **consideration stage** is often the hardest for marketers to influence. At this stage, customers actively compare brands, read reviews, and evaluate features before deciding. Unlike **awareness** or **interest**, where content can spark curiosity, consideration requires deeper trust, clear differentiation, and proof of value. Many digital marketing efforts fail here because brands rely on generic, copy-paste content, basic Canva® designs or AI-generated posts without strategic thought. For instance, a number of e-commerce brands using AI translation for product descriptions have ended up with awkward or misleading content, causing customer confusion or backlash. Vodafone®, too, experienced a mistranslation blunder in social media campaigns, demonstrating that even big brands can falter.

To stand out and influence customers at this stage, marketers need to focus on creativity, relevance and social proof. For example, Zomato® and Swiggy® create engaging Instagram reels and posts showcasing real customer experiences and behind-the-scenes stories, which make their service memorable and trustworthy. A handmade jewellery brand could post short videos showing the crafting process or feature testimonials from happy buyers, providing authenticity and a reason for the customer to choose their product over competitors. Similarly, Amazon® and Flipkart® use personalized recommendations and detailed product reviews to help customers in their evaluation, effectively guiding them towards conversion.

Tip: The consideration stage demands more than just basic content. It requires thoughtful, authentic, and customer-focused communication. Marketers should combine creativity, data insights, and social proof to influence decisions effectively while using AI cautiously to avoid errors that could harm brand credibility.

Creating a Buyer Persona

A buyer persona is an imaginary profile that represents your ideal customer based on real data and market research. It goes beyond assumptions by using actual information, such as age, gender, income level, location, profession, interests, values, lifestyle preferences, and online behaviours. This profile helps marketers understand who their target audience is, what they care about, and how they make purchasing decisions.

Creating a buyer persona is like building a character in a story. It gives marketers a clearer picture of the customer's goals, challenges, motivations, and digital habits. With this understanding, businesses can craft more personalized and effective marketing messages, choose appropriate communication platforms, and develop products or services that better meet customer needs (Heath 2022).

For instance, imagine you are marketing trendy handcrafted jewellery. Your buyer persona might be a 24-year-old woman living in Delhi who follows fashion influencers on Instagram, values uniqueness, and prefers shopping online during seasonal sales. Knowing this, marketers can focus their efforts on social media platforms like Instagram or Pinterest, use influencer collaborations, and offer time-limited deals to attract her attention.

The process of creating a buyer persona typically involves:

- **Collecting data** through surveys, interviews, website analytics, and social media insights.
- **Identifying common traits** and patterns in customer behaviour.
- **Organizing details** into a fictional profile that includes name, age, goals, pain points, buying motivations, and preferred content formats.
- **Updating regularly** as customer trends and digital behaviours evolve over time.

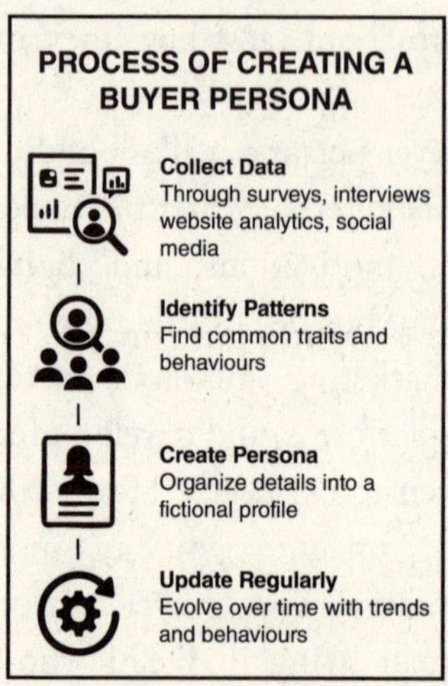

Fig. 2.2: Buyer persona process

Why Do Marketers Use Buyer Personas?

In digital marketing, success does not come from trying to reach everyone. Instead, it comes from reaching the right people with the right message at the right time. This is where buyer personas become valuable. A well-developed buyer persona helps marketers focus their strategies by understanding the preferences, challenges, and behaviours of their ideal customers (Revella 2015).

Buyer personas serve as a strategic tool that guides the entire marketing process. They allow businesses to create more personalized, targeted, and efficient campaigns. Here are some key reasons why marketers rely on buyer personas:

- **To create effective ad copy and content:** When marketers know who they are talking to, they can adapt their tone, language, and messaging to fit the audience. For example, writing for a college student requires a different approach from writing for a corporate manager. As Pulizzi (2014) explains, content must align with the customer's interests and needs to be truly impactful.

- **To choose the right platform for communication:** Understanding customer habits helps marketers choose where to advertise and engage. A student in her early twenties might be active on Instagram or Pinterest, while a business executive is more likely to use LinkedIn. Heath (2022) notes that selecting the appropriate platform based on persona insights increases the effectiveness of digital campaigns and ensures that the message reaches the intended audience.
- **To design cost-effective marketing campaigns:** Marketing to a defined audience prevents wasted effort and budget. Instead of showing ads to the general population, marketers can target specific segments that are more likely to convert. It emphasizes that buyer personas reduce guesswork and help allocate resources more efficiently, improving return on investment.
- **To offer the right product or service:** A deep understanding of what customers value, whether it is quality, affordability, uniqueness, or convenience, enables businesses to customize their products or services accordingly. According to Heath (2022), aligning product features and pricing with persona expectations leads to greater customer satisfaction and loyalty.

Example: Buyer Persona for a Handmade Jewellery Brand

Let's take the example of a brand that sells handmade jewellery. Here's what a basic buyer persona might look like:

Fig. 2.3: Products that may appeal to Siya

- **Name:** Siya
- **Age:** 24
- **Location:** Ghaziabad
- **Profession:** Fashion design student
- **Interests:** Indie fashion, Instagram trends, online shopping
- **Online Habits:** Active on Instagram and Pinterest, follows influencers
- **Goals:** Wants to stand out with unique, stylish accessories
- **Challenges:** Doesn't like mass-produced jewellery, prefers custom or personalized items

Now imagine you are the brand owner. You can ask yourself questions like these:

- Would Siya enjoy a behind-the-scenes video showing how the jewellery is made?
- Should we offer her a limited-time student discount in an Instagram ad?
- Can we show a short testimonial from another fashion student who bought from us?

These small but focused efforts make the brand more relatable and appealing to your target audience. It increases the chances of engagement, trust, and ultimately, sales.

Tip: How Marketers Predict Buyer Behaviour Accurately

A buyer persona is not based on guesswork or the marketer's or seller's personal biases. Marketers step into the customer's shoes *after* collecting real behavioural cues, often gathered from some of these:

- Social media insights (posts with the highest engagement)
- Customer reviews and feedback
- Polls/questions asked by followers
- Website and sales data (top-selling products, repeat purchases)
- Competitor content that performs well

How Many Buyer Personas Should You Create?

If you are just starting out, creating one to three buyer personas is usually enough. Each persona should represent a different segment of your audience.

For example, the same handmade jewellery brand might have the following personas:

- **Persona 1:** Young girls who buy jewellery for themselves
- **Persona 2:** Parents who purchase jewellery as gifts for their daughters
- **Persona 3:** Working professionals looking for elegant office wear accessories

By preparing separate content or campaigns for each group, your brand can connect more deeply with different types of buyers. As your business grows, you can add more personas or update them based on new data.

Additional Tips for Creating Buyer Personas

- Use free surveys or Google Forms to collect basic customer details.
- Observe comments, reviews, and FAQs to understand what customers care about.
- Check your social media insights to find your audience's age, location, and activity.
- Start simple. Even a basic persona is better than none.

In summary, creating a buyer persona helps you step into the shoes of your customer. It allows you to market smarter, not harder. When you truly understand who your customer is, where they are, and what they care about, you can build better products, run more effective campaigns, and form stronger relationships. In digital marketing, this is one of the most powerful tools for success.

Role of Personalization

Personalization in digital marketing refers to the practice of delivering relevant messages, content, and offers to individual customers based on their interests, behaviour, and preferences. Rather than using the same message for everyone, brands now rely on data-driven insights to tailor their communication to meet the specific needs of each user.

For instance, when a customer browses for running shoes on an e-commerce site, they may later receive an email showcasing similar products or see ads for sportswear on Instagram. These personalized interactions are made possible through technologies such as cookies, customer relationship management (CRM) systems, and artificial intelligence (AI).

This personalized approach helps build deeper customer relationships. When people receive content that feels relevant to them, they are more likely to respond positively. It enhances trust and increases the chances of conversion. Personalization also improves customer retention. When customers feel seen and understood, they are more likely to return to the brand for future purchases. In today's competitive digital environment, this approach not only improves engagement but also contributes to long-term loyalty and business growth (Heath 2022).

Everyday Examples of Personalization:

- When you search for *Flight from Delhi to Ahmedabad* on Google and you later see ads for air tickets in that range on websites or social media, that is personalization.
- When Amazon recommends products based on your past searches or purchases, it is using your behaviour to show what you might want next.
- When a clothing brand sends you a discount code on your birthday, that is a personalized message designed to make you feel special and encourage a purchase.

These examples show how personalization works in everyday life and why customers respond well to it.

Why Is Personalization Important?

- **Better user experience:** Customers feel more connected when the content they see matches their needs and interests.

- **Higher conversions:** People are more likely to take action, such as buying a product or signing up, when offers match what they are already looking for.
- **Reduced wasted budget:** Businesses save money by focusing only on the people who are most likely to respond.
- **Improved loyalty:** Customers are more likely to return to a brand that understands their preferences and communicates personally.

How Do Marketers Use Personalization?

In today's digital world, personalization is not just a bonus. It is something customers expect. People want brands to understand their choices and give them meaningful options, not random messages. That is why personalization has become a powerful and essential part of digital marketing. Marketers who use data smartly to personalize their campaigns can connect better with their audience, improve engagement, and grow faster in today's competitive online environment. Here are some common methods:

- **Ads based on past activity:** Marketers display ads to users based on their previous browsing behaviour, such as products they searched for, pages they visited, or items they clicked on. This helps re-engage interested customers who did not complete a purchase.
- **Targeted emails:** Businesses send personalized emails that include product suggestions, special offers, or reminders based on the customer's past shopping activity.

For example, an email recommending items related to a recent purchase.

- **Location-based offers:** Brands use the customer's geographic location to send timely and relevant messages. For instance, showing lunch deals from nearby restaurants during midday hours or promoting raincoats in areas experiencing monsoon weather.
- **Product recommendations:** E-commerce websites suggest related or complementary products by analysing what the customer has viewed, added to their cart, or purchased before. This technique not only improves user experience but also increases the average order value.

How Personalization Can Go Wrong

Personalization can go wrong when marketers rely on inaccurate, excessive, or irrelevant customer data. When a customer receives recommendations that do not match their interests, or when a brand uses information that feels too personal, the experience becomes uncomfortable rather than helpful. Overly frequent personalized messages can also make customers feel pressured or watched. These mistakes can reduce trust as customers may believe their data is being mishandled or used without proper consent. Once trust declines, customers may stop engaging with the brand or hesitate to share any further information.

Quick Bytes

- Digital buying behaviour refers to how customers search, compare, and make purchases online.

- Customers typically follow a digital journey: Search, Compare, Engage, Decide, and Share.
- Marketers need to understand this behaviour to create more effective content and advertising.
- The customer journey includes five key stages: Awareness, Interest, Consideration, Conversion, and Post-purchase Follow-Up.
- A buyer persona is a detailed profile of the ideal customer used to guide targeted marketing strategies.
- Personalization involves showing relevant content based on user data, which boosts engagement and customer loyalty.
- Using digital tools and customer insights wisely leads to stronger marketing outcomes and better customer experiences.

Self-Assessment Questions *(For Revision and Reflection)*

1. Why do you think understanding digital buying behaviour is more important today than it was ten years ago?
2. If you were creating a buyer persona for an online bookstore, what details would you include, and why?
3. How can personalization go wrong in digital marketing, and what impact might it have on customer trust?
4. In your opinion, which stage of the digital customer journey is the hardest for marketers to influence, and why?

5. Do you agree that personalization and buyer personas can reduce marketing costs while improving results?

References

1. Baymard Institute, *Checkout Usability*, 2023.
2. David C. Edelman and Marc Singer, 'Competing on Customer Journeys', *Harvard Business Review* 93, No. 11 (2015): 88–100.
3. Annmarie Heath, *Digital Marketing Strategy: An Integrated Approach to Online Marketing* (London: Kogan Page, 2022).
4. Philip Kotler, Hermawan Kartajaya, and Iwan Setiawan, *Marketing 5.0: Technology for Humanity* (Hoboken, NJ: Wiley, 2021).
5. Joe Pulizzi, *Epic Content Marketing: How to Tell a Different Story, Break Through the Clutter, and Win More Customers by Marketing Less* (New York: McGraw-Hill Education, 2014).
6. Adele Revella, *Buyer Personas: How to Gain Insight into Your Customer's Expectations, Align Your Marketing Strategies, and Win More Business* (Hoboken, NJ: Wiley, 2015).

Chapter 3

Building an Online Presence

In the present digital age, having an online presence is not just an option; it is a necessity. Whether you are a local shop owner, a freelancer, a start-up founder, or part of a large organization, your visibility on the internet significantly affects how potential customers discover, understand, engage with, and remember your brand. An online presence refers to how your brand appears across various digital platforms. This includes your website, social media profiles, search engine results, online directories, customer reviews, and listings on e-commerce platforms such as Amazon, Flipkart, or Etsy. Every point of interaction, from a Google search result to an Instagram post, shapes the way people perceive your business (Chaffey and Smith 2017).

The stronger your online presence, the more likely you are to build trust, attract new customers, and retain existing ones. According to Ryan (2016), today's customers often research a product or service online before making a purchase. This means that if your business is not visible online or if the information available is unclear or outdated, you may lose opportunities to competitors who are more digitally active. A strong online presence also improves your search engine visibility, enhances brand credibility, and supports consistent communication with your target audience. It allows businesses to deliver valuable content, respond to customer queries, share updates, and drive traffic to their website or online store.

Importance of a Website

A website is a vital part of your digital presence. It functions as your permanent online office or storefront, available to anyone, anywhere, at any time. Unlike physical locations that close at specific hours, a website is accessible 24 hours a day, 7 days a week, allowing people to learn about your business at their convenience. For many customers, the website is often the first point of contact with a brand. It provides essential information, such as what the business offers, how to get in touch, and why it might be trustworthy. A professional, easy-to-navigate website can help build credibility and make a strong first impression.

Additionally, the website acts as the central point that connects other digital marketing activities. Whether a person finds your business through a social media post, an online ad, or a search engine result, they are likely to visit your website for more information before deciding. This makes the website an important space for converting interest into action, such as a purchase, registration, or enquiry.

According to Kingsnorth (2019), a well-structured website can support business growth and customer engagement, but its effectiveness depends on content quality, user experience, and how well it is integrated with other marketing efforts.

Why Does Every Business Need a Website?

- A website helps build trust and establishes credibility, especially for first-time visitors.
- Customers can easily find important information, such as your location, product or service details, pricing, business hours, and contact information, and can even make a purchase directly.
- You have complete control over the content, layout, and messaging, unlike social media platforms, which are governed by third-party algorithms and rules.
- A website improves your visibility in Google search results, increasing the chances of being discovered by potential customers online.

Note: Even a basic website with just three to five pages, such as Home, About Us, Products or Services, and Contact Us, is a strong starting point.

Domain, Hosting, and CMS Basics

To create a website, you need three essential components: a domain name, a hosting service, and a content management system (CMS). Understanding these basics will help you get started with confidence.

1. **Domain name:** This is your website's address on the internet. A good domain name helps your audience find and recall your site more easily. For example, www.myntra.com. It is what people type into their browser to visit your site.

   When choosing a domain name, make sure it is

- short and easy to remember,
- closely related to your brand or business name, and
- simple to spell and pronounce.

2. **Hosting:** Web hosting is a service that stores all the files, images, videos, and data that make up your website and makes them accessible to users through the internet. You can think of hosting as renting a space on the internet where your website lives. Without hosting, your website cannot be viewed online. Whenever someone types your domain name into a browser, the hosting server delivers your website content to their device. Hosting ensures your website loads properly and stays online without interruptions.

   There are several types of hosting services, and each is designed to meet different needs and budgets:

   - **Shared hosting:** This is the most affordable and beginner-friendly option. Your website shares server resources with other websites. It works well for small websites, personal blogs, or businesses just starting out. However, since resources are shared, performance may slow down during high traffic periods.

     > **Tip:** In shared hosting, only the server space is shared and not the domain name. Each website continues to operate with its own unique domain address, even when hosted on the same server.

   - **Virtual Private Server hosting (VPS):** In VPS hosting, your website shares a server with others, but you are given a separate section with dedicated resources. It offers better speed, security, and control compared to shared hosting. This is ideal for growing websites that need more stability and flexibility.

- **Dedicated hosting:** With dedicated hosting, your website gets an entire server to itself. This provides maximum control, speed, and security. It is best suited for large websites or e-commerce platforms with heavy traffic and custom requirements. It is also the most expensive option.
- **Cloud hosting:** Cloud hosting uses a network of servers, offering high reliability and scalability. If one server fails, another instantly takes over. This is a good option for businesses that expect traffic spikes or need consistent uptime.

Note: When choosing a hosting plan, consider factors such as your budget, website size, expected traffic, and whether you need technical support. For most beginners, shared hosting is a practical and affordable starting point.

3. **Content management system (CMS):** A CMS is a software application that allows users to create, manage, and update website content without needing to write or understand programming code. It simplifies the entire process of building a website, making it accessible even to those with no technical background.

Instead of writing complex hypertext markup language (HTML) or cascading style sheets (CSS) code, users can use a visual interface to design pages, upload images or videos and publish blog posts. Most CMS platforms offer drag-and-drop features, ready-to-use templates, and plug-in support, making it easy to customize the look and functionality of a website.

A CMS usually has two main parts:

- **The front end:** This is what visitors see when they visit your website, your homepage, product pages, contact form, etc.
- **The back end (dashboard):** This is where you, as the website owner or admin, control the website's content, settings, layout, and updates.

Some beginner-friendly CMS platforms include:

- **WordPress®:** The most popular CMS globally. It is open-source, highly flexible and supports thousands of themes and plug-ins. Suitable for blogs, business websites, and e-commerce through integrations like WooCommerce.

Fig. 3.1: CMS platforms

- **Wix®:** Known for its simple drag-and-drop interface. Great for small businesses, freelancers, or personal portfolios. No coding skills are needed, and it offers built-in hosting.
- **Shopify®:** Designed specifically for e-commerce. It allows users to create online stores, manage inventory, process payments, and run promotions with ease. Ideal for businesses focused on selling products online.
- **Squarespace® and Weebly®:** Both offer beginner-friendly tools and elegant templates. They are good choices for creative professionals, small stores, and service-based websites.

Each platform offers different features, so the right choice depends on your website goals and level of technical comfort. For general use and flexibility, WordPress is a strong choice. For online selling, Shopify is often the best option.

Example: Creating a website is like building a house

- First, you choose a location for your house. In the digital world, this is your domain name – that is, the address people use to find your website.
- Second, you need to buy land where the house will be built. This is like purchasing web hosting, which provides the space where your website files are stored.
- Third, you design and furnish the rooms of your house. This is where the CMS helps you create pages, upload images and organize content without needing technical skills.

Must-Have Features on Websites

If you are just starting out, your website does not need to be complex or expensive. Several free tools are available, such as Wix, WordPress, and Shopify Website Builder. These are suitable for students, small businesses, or beginners working with limited budgets. They offer simple templates and easy-to-use features without requiring any technical skills. However, it should include the following essential features to provide a smooth and effective user experience:

- **Mobile-friendly design:** Your website should look good and function well on all screen sizes, including smartphones, tablets, and desktops. A website that adjusts its layout automatically based on the device is called a responsive website.
- **Fast loading speed:** Websites that take too long to load often lose visitors. To improve speed, use lightweight designs, optimize image sizes, and reduce unnecessary CSS or code-heavy elements.
- **Clear navigation:** Users should be able to find what they are looking for easily. Use a clean, simple menu and a well-organized layout to help visitors move around your website without confusion.
- **Call-to-action (CTA) buttons:** Encourage users to take specific actions with clearly labelled buttons like Buy Now, Sign Up, or Contact Us. These buttons guide the visitor towards your desired goals.
- **Basic SEO set-up:** Make sure your website is searchable on platforms like Google. Use relevant keywords, proper

page titles, meta descriptions, and headers to help search engines understand and rank your site.

Introduction to Content Marketing

Once your website is live, the next step is to fill it with valuable content that educates, entertains, or solves problems for your audience. This practice is called content marketing. It involves creating and sharing materials such as blogs, videos, infographics, podcasts, how-to guides, and Frequently Asked Questions (FAQs) to attract and engage readers without directly promoting products (Pulizzi 2014).

Content marketing builds long-term relationships with your audience by delivering real value. For instance, a helpful blog post or a clear tutorial can earn trust, prompt visitors to revisit your site and increase the likelihood of conversion (Baltes 2015). It moves the focus away from direct selling and towards establishing your brand as a credible source. Effective content marketing also enhances your visibility on search engines. When Google recognizes that your content addresses common user queries clearly and thoroughly, it may rank your pages higher in search results. This organic traffic brings ongoing benefits without ongoing ad costs.

Recent research suggests that today's content marketing landscape emphasizes interactive formats and user-generated content. Studies also highlight the importance of personalized, data-driven strategies to keep content relevant and engaging (MDPI 2024; Kentico 2024). According to a 2023 report, these trends help businesses connect with their audience in more meaningful ways and support digital transformation goals.

Why Content Marketing Matters?

Today's internet users are no longer responsive to constant advertising. Instead, they seek useful information, problem-solving content, and meaningful experiences. Businesses that consistently provide such content build a foundation of trust, which leads to increased loyalty and higher conversion rates for paying customers. Content marketing positions your brand as a trusted advisor rather than a mere salesperson. When users find your posts, videos, or guides genuinely helpful, they are more likely to remember your brand, recommend it to others, and eventually choose your products or services. In fact, 68 per cent of consumers report feeling more positive about a brand after interacting with its content (Worldmetrics 2024).

A powerful benefit of content marketing is improved search engine visibility. Quality content that answers real questions, solves problems, or offers valuable insights often ranks higher in Google results. This boosts organic traffic without ongoing ad spend and supports long-term website growth. In the digital landscape, trust and personalization are crucial. The Adobe 2022 Trust Report shows that 70 per cent of consumers say well-timed, relevant content significantly increases their trust in a brand. Conversely, 72 per cent say poor personalization can erode trust (Adobe 2022). Delivering consistent, personalized content helps strengthen customer connections, foster loyalty, and encourage repeat purchases.

Example of content marketing: A small skincare startup launched its website in 2022, but for the first six months it received very low traffic and only a handful of orders. Instead of increasing ads, the business started publishing weekly content such as 'how to choose the right cleanser', 'home remedies for dry skin,' and seasonal skincare tips. These posts answered common user queries and linked to relevant products on the website. Within four months, the blog became the biggest traffic source for the business, organic visits increased by over 200%, and monthly sales nearly tripled. Customers shared the articles on social media and returned to the website for buying decisions because they trusted the brand's helpful content rather than paid advertising.

Basics of Visual Content, Blogs, and Landing Pages

As a beginner, you can start with a few simple yet powerful types of content to engage your audience and grow your online presence. Here are four key content formats to focus on:

1. **Blog post:**
   - Short, informative articles published on your website that address topics your target audience is interested in.
   - They help educate readers, answer common questions, and improve your visibility on search engines.

   Examples: *5 Tips for Glowing Skin, How to Start an Online Business in India*

2. **Visual content:**
   - Includes infographics, images, charts, and videos that explain concepts or entertain viewers in a visual format.

- Visual content is more engaging and easier to understand than text alone.
- Tools like Canva® and Invideo® make it simple to create professional-quality visuals, even for beginners.

3. **Landing pages:**
    - Standalone web pages focused on a single goal, such as promoting a product, service, campaign, or offer.
    - These pages are designed with a clear CTA, such as Buy Now, Download Free Guide, or Sign Up Today.
    - A well-designed landing page helps convert visitors into leads or customers.
4. **Social media content:**
    - Sharing your blogs, videos, graphics, and updates on platforms like Facebook®, Instagram®, X® (formerly Twitter), YouTube®, and LinkedIn® helps amplify your message.
    - Social media increases your content's reach and drives more traffic back to your website.
    - It also helps you interact with your audience and build a community around your brand.

Key Benefits of Content Marketing: Content marketing offers long-term value and plays a vital role in building a strong online presence. However, it usually takes more time than paid advertising to show noticeable results. In most cases, businesses begin to see the impact after three to six months of consistent content creation and publishing. Although the results are not immediate, content marketing remains one of the most cost-effective and sustainable strategies for business growth. Unlike paid ads, which stop generating results as soon as the budget ends, valuable content continues to attract traffic, build trust, and generate leads for months or even years after it is published. Content marketing is not a shortcut to success but a strategic investment. When it is combined with search engine optimization, social media marketing and email campaigns, it can lead to significant and lasting growth for your business.

Here are the key benefits of content marketing:

- **Increases website traffic:** High-quality and relevant content attracts more visitors to your website and encourages them to stay longer, explore more pages and return in the future.
- **Improves search engine ranking:** Regularly publishing keyword-rich content helps your website appear higher in search engine results. This increases your visibility and drives organic (unpaid) traffic.

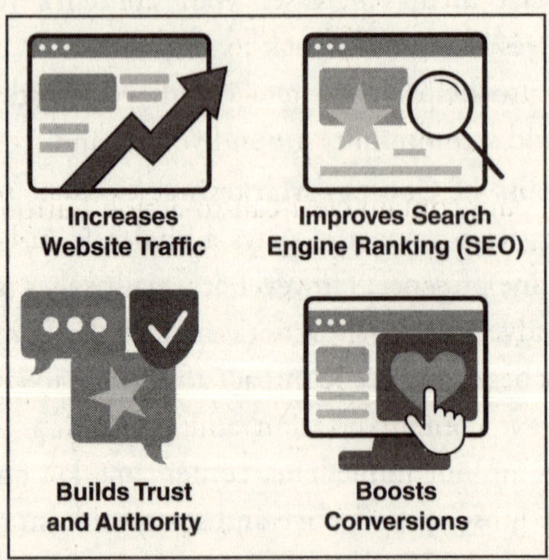

Fig. 3.2: Benefits of content marketing

- **Builds trust and authority:** When users find your content useful, educational, or insightful, they begin to see your brand as a credible source. Over time, this builds trust and positions your business as an authority in your niche.
- **Boosts conversions:** Engaged visitors are more likely to take meaningful actions such as signing up for a newsletter, downloading a free resource, making a purchase, or filling out a contact form.

Quick Bytes

- A strong online presence makes your business visible, trustworthy, and accessible 24/7.
- A website acts as your digital home. Even a basic website can build credibility.
- To build a website, you need a domain name (web address), hosting (online storage), and a CMS (website-building tool).
- Beginner-friendly CMS platforms include WordPress, Wix, and Shopify.
- A good website should be mobile-friendly, fast, easy to navigate, and contain clear call-to-action buttons.
- Content marketing involves creating helpful blogs, videos, infographics, and more to attract and engage your audience.
- Great content builds trust increases web traffic, and supports your overall digital marketing strategy.

Self-Assessment Questions *(For Revision and Reflection)*

1. Why do you think some businesses grow faster online than others even when they sell similar products?
2. Imagine a shop with no website. Would you trust it as much as one with a proper online presence? Why or why not?
3. If you were starting your first website, what kind of hosting service would you choose and why?
4. Think of a website you enjoy using. What features make it easy and enjoyable, and how could beginners learn from it?
5. When was the last time a blog, video, or article convinced you to try a product? What made that content effective?

References

1. Adobe, *2022 Trust Report: Customer Trust Is Earned or Broken with Every Experience* (Adobe, 2022).
2. L. P. Baltes, 'Content Marketing—the Fundamental Tool of Digital Marketing,' *Bulletin of the Transilvania University of Brașov. Series V: Economic Sciences* 8, no. 2 (2015): 111–118.
3. Dave Chaffey and P. R. Smith, *Digital Marketing Excellence: Planning, Optimizing and Integrating Online Marketing*, 6th ed. (London: Routledge, 2017).
4. Kentico, '10 Content Marketing Trends to Look Out for in 2025' (Kentico, 2024).

5. Simon Kingsnorth, *Digital Marketing Strategy: An Integrated Approach to Online Marketing* (London: Kogan Page, 2019).
6. MDPI, 'Content Marketing in the Digital Transformation Era: Trends and Best Practices', *Proceedings* 101 (2024): 7.
7. Joe Pulizzi, *Epic Content Marketing: How to Tell a Different Story, Break through the Clutter and Win More Customers by Marketing Less* (New York: McGraw-Hill Education, 2014).
8. Damian Ryan, *Understanding Digital Marketing: Marketing Strategies for Engaging the Digital Generation*, 4th ed. (London: Kogan Page, 2016).
9. Worldmetrics, 'Consumer Perception and Brand Positivity: Content Marketing Statistics' (Worldmetrics, 2024).

Chapter 4

Search Engine Optimization

Search engine optimization (SEO) is the practice of enhancing a website's visibility in organic (non-paid) search engine results. When users search for information on platforms like Google, Bing, or YouTube, SEO ensures that your content naturally appears among the top results without having to rely on paid advertising (Fishkin 2015). For example, if someone types 'Best budget phones under ₹15,000' into Google, the websites that appear on the first page are likely using effective SEO strategies. These strategies signal to search engines that their content is relevant, credible, and valuable for that specific query.

SEO involves several important practices, such as selecting the right keywords, writing helpful and well-structured content, improving page load speed, optimizing mobile responsiveness, and using proper meta tags and headings. Each of these factors contributes to better rankings and a more user-friendly experience (Moz 2024). What makes SEO particularly valuable is its long-term impact. Unlike paid ads, which disappear as soon as the budget is used up, a well-optimized website can continue to attract visitors for weeks or even months. According to HubSpot (2023), SEO is one of the most cost-effective ways to build digital presence and trust, especially for small businesses and start-ups.

The Importance of SEO

- **Increased visibility**: Research shows that most users click on one of the top results on the first page of Google. If your website ranks higher, it is more likely to attract clicks and visits from potential customers.
- **Cost-effective traffic**: Unlike paid ads, SEO generates organic traffic, meaning you do not pay each time someone visits your site. Over time, this makes SEO one of the most budget-friendly digital strategies for sustained traffic generation.
- **Builds trust and credibility**: Users tend to trust websites that appear naturally in search results more than those marked as 'sponsored' or 'ads'. Ranking organically increases the perceived authority of your brand.
- **Long-term results**: A well-optimized webpage can continue to rank and attract traffic for weeks or even months without requiring ongoing investment. This makes SEO a strategic tool for long-term digital success.
- **Enhanced user experience**: SEO is not just about keywords. It also includes improving site speed, mobile responsiveness, content clarity, and navigation, all of which contribute to a better experience for your visitors.

Types of SEO

To improve your website's visibility on search engines, it is important to understand the three main types of SEO. Each type focuses on a different aspect of optimization and plays a unique role in helping your site perform better online. There are three main types of SEO that everyone should know:

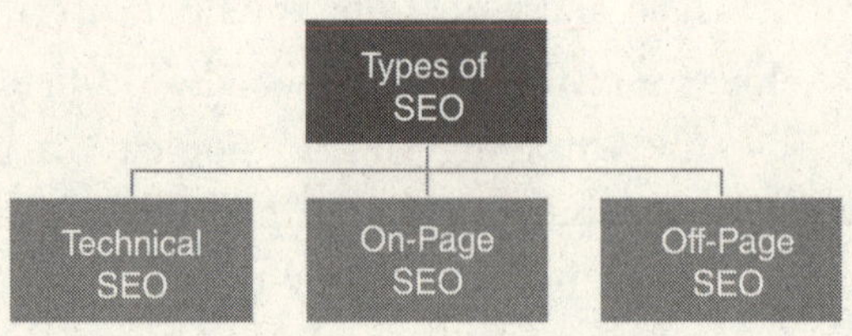

Fig. 4.1: Types of SEO

Technical SEO

Technical SEO refers to the behind-the-scenes improvements that help search engines crawl, index, and understand your website efficiently. This includes optimizing the structure, speed, security and mobile-friendliness of the website. These improvements ensure that your content is accessible and understandable to search engine bots, which increases the chances of ranking higher on search engine results pages (SERPs).

Unlike on-page SEO, which focuses on visible content, such as keywords and headings, and off-page SEO, which deals with backlinks and online reputation, technical SEO addresses the foundational elements of a website. Its goal is to create a seamless experience for both users and search engines by removing any technical barriers to indexing and ranking (Berman and Katona 2020).

Tip:

- **Crawling:** Search engines use bots (also called spiders) to discover new and updated pages on the web. These bots follow links from known pages to find content.
- **Indexing:** Once a page is crawled, the search engine stores and organizes the content in its database (index). Indexed pages are eligible to appear in search results.
- **Ranking:** When a user searches, the search engine evaluates all indexed pages using algorithms that consider relevance, quality, and user experience. Pages are then ranked on the SERPs based on how well they satisfy the user's query.

Key takeaway: Technical SEO ensures that your site can be easily crawled and indexed, which is essential for your pages to be considered for ranking.

Even with high-quality content, a website can struggle to rank if technical issues exist. Let's look at the role of technical SEO point by point once more:

1. **Improves crawlability and indexing:** Search engines use bots to crawl and index web pages. If your site is not structured properly or includes blocked resources, search engines may miss important pages.
2. **Enhances page speed and load time:** Fast-loading websites provide a better user experience and are prioritized by search engines. A delay of even one second in page load time can reduce conversions by 7 per cent.

3. **Boosts mobile friendliness:** With mobile-first indexing, Google predominantly uses the mobile version of content for indexing and ranking. A mobile-friendly site is essential for SEO performance.
4. **Reduces site errors:** Technical SEO helps identify and fix 404 errors, broken links and redirect loops issues that hurt both user experience and search engine rankings (Moz 2023).
5. **Secures your website (HTTPS):** Security is a ranking factor. Websites with HTTPS encryption are favoured by search engines and trusted more by users.
6. **Enables better structured data:** Technical SEO allows the implementation of schema mark-up, which helps search engines understand your content better and display rich results such as star ratings and product information (Fishkin 2015).
7. **Supports long-term SEO strategy:** Unlike quick-fix SEO tricks, technical SEO builds a strong foundation for scalable, long-term organic traffic growth.

Key elements of Technical SEO

Here are the most important components of technical SEO:

1. **Website speed (page load time)**
   - A slow website leads to a poor user experience.
   - Google prefers fast-loading websites.

   Tip: *Compress images, use a fast-hosting service and reduce unnecessary plug-ins or code.*

Example: If your homepage takes eight seconds to load, visitors may leave before it opens. But if it loads in two to three seconds, they're more likely to stay and explore.

2. **Mobile-Friendliness**
   - Most users now browse on mobile devices.
   - Google uses 'mobile-first indexing', meaning it looks at the mobile version first.

Tip: *Use a responsive design that adapts to different screen sizes.*

Example: A clothing website that displays clearly on both desktop and mobile devices will rank better than one that's hard to navigate on a phone.

3. **Secure Sockets Layer (SSL) certificate**
   - A secure website uses HTTPS (not HTTP).
   - It protects user data and builds trust.

Tip: *Install an SSL certificate (many web hosting services offer it for free).*

Example: A website with a green padlock and HTTPS in the address bar gives users confidence to browse or buy safely.

4. **Extensible Mark-Up Language (XML) Sitemap**
   - A sitemap is a file that lists all the important pages of your site.
   - It helps search engines crawl and index your pages efficiently.

***Tip*:** *Use tools like Yoast SEO (for WordPress) to create and submit a sitemap to Google Search Console (Formerly Google Webmaster).*

Example: An online store with hundreds of products can use a sitemap to ensure Google indexes all product pages. It looks like a book's table of contents.

5. **Robots.txt File**
   - This file tells search engines which pages *should* or *should not* be crawled.
   - Useful for keeping private or duplicate pages out of search results.

   Tip*: *Make sure you haven't accidentally blocked important pages in robots.txt.

6. **Fixing Crawl Errors**
   - Sometimes, pages return errors (like '404 Not Found') or are blocked.
   - These errors can prevent Google from accessing or ranking your pages.

   Tip*: *Check crawl errors regularly in Google Search Console and fix broken links or redirect missing pages.

7. **Canonical Tags**
   - These tags tell search engines which version of a page is the 'main' one.
   - Helps avoid duplicate content issues.

   Tip*: *Use canonical tags on pages with similar or identical content.

   Example: If your product appears under two categories, the canonical tag ensures only one version is indexed.

Technical SEO makes sure your website runs smoothly, loads fast, is mobile-friendly, and is easy for Google to read.

It improves your chances of ranking higher without needing new content or backlinks.

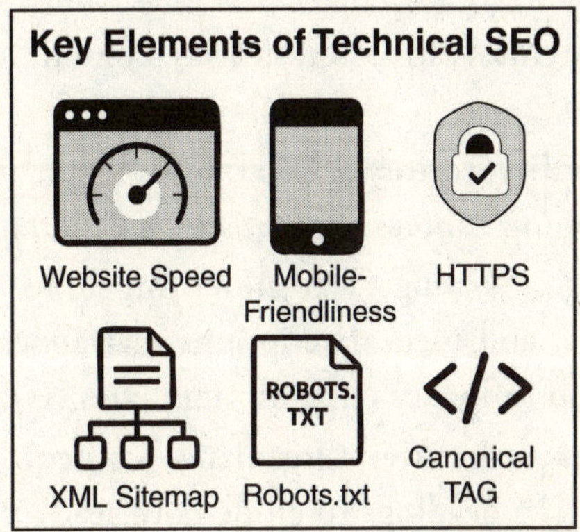

Fig. 4.2: Key Elements of Technical SEO

On-Page SEO

On-Page SEO refers to all the activities you perform directly on your website to help search engines like Google understand your content better. It involves optimizing the text, images, structure, and overall experience of individual web pages to improve visibility in search engine results.

With a focus on external links and promotion, on-page SEO gives you full control. It ensures that your content is relevant, your website is easy to navigate, and that both users and search engines can understand what your pages are about.

Key components of on-page SEO include:

- **Keyword optimization:** Using relevant keywords naturally in your content, headings, and meta tags so search engines can connect your content with search queries.
- **High-quality content:** Creating original, informative, and engaging content that satisfies user intent.
- **Meta tags:** Writing clear and compelling meta titles, meta tags, and meta descriptions that appear in search results and influence click-through rates (CTR).
- **Headings structure:** Organizing content using H1, H2, and H3 headings to guide both readers and search engines through your page.
- **Internal linking:** Connecting your content with other pages on your site to help users and search engines discover related content.
- **Image optimization:** Using descriptive file names and alt text for images, which improves accessibility and helps search engines understand visual content.
- **Mobile friendliness and readability:** Ensuring your site displays well on all devices. That content is easy to read with an appropriate font size, spacing, and layout.

Why Is On-Page SEO Important?

On-Page SEO plays a foundational role in digital marketing. Without proper on-page optimization, even high-quality content may not be discoverable by your target audience. Effective on-page SEO not only attracts visitors but also keeps them engaged and encourages action. This makes it a critical part of any successful SEO strategy.

Here's why on-page SEO matters:

- **Improves search engine visibility:** Search engines use your on-page content to determine what your page is about and how relevant it is to a user's query. Well-optimized pages are more likely to appear higher in search results.
- **Enhances user experience:** A clean layout, logical structure, and useful content make it easier for users to find the information they need, which reduces bounce rates and encourages return visits.
- **Increases organic traffic:** As your rankings improve, more people are likely to click on your page, bringing in visitors without the need for paid advertising.
- **Boosts engagement and conversions:** Engaging content with a clear call to action (CTAs) can lead visitors to take specific steps, such as signing up for a newsletter or making a purchase.
- **Supports long-term growth:** On-page SEO helps build authority over time. When your site consistently delivers valuable content that ranks well, it establishes your credibility in your niche.

Example of On-Page SEO in Action

Imagine you are writing a blog post titled 'How to Take Care of Oily Skin in Summer'. To make sure the post is optimized for search engines and easy for readers to follow, you would apply several on-page SEO techniques:

- **Use target keywords naturally:** Choose a keyword phrase such as *oily skin care tips* and include it in your blog title, subheadings, and throughout the main content. This tells search engines what your article is about.
- **Write an SEO-friendly title:** Use a clear and relevant title like 'How to Take Care of Oily Skin in Summer: 6 Simple Tips'. This makes the topic obvious to readers and encourages clicks.
- **Add a compelling meta description:** Create a summary like 'Learn 6 simple and affordable skincare tips for oily skin during hot weather to keep your skin fresh and oil-free'. This appears below the title in search results and helps users decide to click.
- **Use proper headings (H1, H2, H3...):** Break your content into sections using headings; for example, 'Tip 1: Use a gentle face wash', 'Tip 2: Avoid heavy creams'. This makes the blog easier to scan and improves readability.
- **Optimize images:** Include a photo of a product like a face wash and use descriptive alt text such as 'Face wash suitable for oily skin'. This helps visually impaired users and improves image SEO.
- **Use internal links:** Link to another relevant post on your website, like 'Read more about choosing the right sunscreen for oily skin'. This improves site structure and encourages visitors to explore more content.

- **Create a clean URL:** Use a short and simple web address, such as *yourblog.com/oily-skin-care-tips*. This makes the link easier to share and understand.

Off-Page SEO

Off-page SEO refers to all the actions you take outside your website to improve its ranking, trustworthiness, and popularity in search engine results. While on-page SEO focuses on content and structure within your website, off-page SEO is about how other websites, platforms, and users interact with your content across the internet.

It is like building your reputation in the digital world. When other websites link to your content or when your work is shared and talked about online, search engines view your site as more useful and trustworthy.

Why Is Off-Page SEO Important?

Off-page SEO is crucial because it helps:

- **Improve your search engine ranking:** High-quality links from other websites act as trust signals for Google and other search engines.
- **Build credibility and authority:** If trusted websites mention or link to your content, your brand appears more reliable to both users and search engines.
- **Increase traffic from other sources:** Social media shares, directory listings, and online mentions can send new visitors to your site.

- **Support long-term online growth:** A strong off-page SEO strategy builds consistent visibility and reputation over time.

Key Components of Off-Page SEO Techniques

1. **Backlinks (inbound links):** Backlinks are links from other websites to your own. Search engines treat them as votes of confidence. The more high-quality backlinks you earn, the more likely your site will rank higher in search results. Focus on getting backlinks from trustworthy and relevant websites.
2. **Social sharing:** When people share your content on platforms like Facebook, Instagram, LinkedIn, or WhatsApp, it increases your visibility and builds brand awareness. Although social signals may not directly affect rankings, they can attract more users and encourage others to link to your content.
3. **Guest blogging:** Writing guest posts for other websites in your niche allows you to showcase your expertise and include a link back to your site. This brings referral traffic, builds backlinks, and connects you with a wider audience.
4. **Influencer mentions:** If a well-known expert or influencer mentions your brand, recommends your product, or shares your link, it improves your credibility and brings more traffic to your site.
5. **Online reviews and business listings:** Positive reviews on Google Business Profile, JustDial, TripAdvisor, and similar platforms improve your local SEO. They also

influence customers who rely on reviews before making decisions. Keeping your listings updated with correct contact information is essential.

6. **Forum participation and commenting:** Contributing to online forums or blog discussions by sharing helpful information can attract visitors to your website. When done appropriately, this creates awareness and builds authority within your niche.

An Example of Off-Page SEO

Imagine you run a website called FitLifeTips.com that offers advice on health and fitness. Here are a few ways off-page SEO could help grow your site:

- **Guest blogging:** You write a blog post for Healthline.com titled '5 Easy Exercises for Beginners' and include a link back to your own site. This provides a valuable backlink from a trusted and popular health platform.
- **Influencer sharing:** A fitness influencer on Instagram shares one of your articles and tags your website. This increases brand exposure and attracts new visitors through social proof.
- **Business listings and reviews:** You list your site on Google Business Profile and receive five-star reviews from satisfied users. This improves your local visibility and builds credibility with potential visitors.
- **Social sharing:** Readers share your blog post titled 'Healthy Indian Breakfast Ideas' on platforms like Facebook and WhatsApp. This drives more traffic to your site and improves your content's popularity online.

All of these are off-page SEO strategies. Although they happen outside your website, they significantly impact how your site is perceived, how much traffic it receives, and how well it ranks in search engine results.

In simple words, all three are important for improving your site's visibility in search results and attracting more visitors to your website.

- **Technical SEO:** Making your website easy for search engines to crawl and index by fixing speed, mobile usability, and site errors.
- **On-page SEO:** Making your website Google and AI-friendly by improving content, keywords, titles, and structure.
- **Off-page SEO:** Building your website's reputation outside by getting backlinks, social shares, and mentions.

Keywords, Meta Tags, and Backlinks in SEO

To build a strong foundation in SEO, it is essential to understand three core elements: keywords, meta tags, and backlinks. These components work together to help your website rank higher in search engine results and attract organic (non-paid) traffic. Each plays a distinct role in improving visibility and helping search engines understand and trust your content. Let's explore each one in detail.

1. Keywords

Keywords are the specific words or phrases that users type into search engines like Google when looking for information, products, or services. These terms reflect what people want to find and are the starting point for most online journeys. For example, if someone searches for *best budget laptops under ₹30,000*, that entire phrase acts as a keyword, signalling that the user is interested in affordable laptop options.

Why Are Keywords Important?

According to Moz (2023), selecting and using the right keywords is one of the most effective ways to improve SEO because it ensures your content aligns with what your audience is actively searching for.

- Keywords act as a bridge between user intent and your content.
- When used effectively, they help search engines understand the purpose of your page and match it with relevant search queries.
- Placing keywords strategically in your content (such as titles, headings, meta descriptions, and body text) increases the chances of your website appearing in search results.

Types of Keywords

- **Short-tail keywords:** Broad, one- or two-word phrases like *laptop*. These are highly competitive.
- **Long-tail keywords:** More specific phrases like *affordable laptops for students in India*. These have less competition and higher conversion potential.

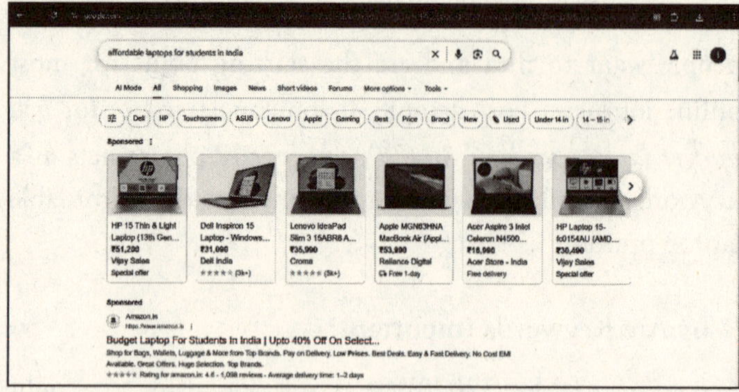

Fig. 4.3: An example of a long-tail keyword

Insider Note: Do not overuse keywords. Insert them naturally into your content so it remains easy to read. This practice is called **keyword optimization** and it helps both search engines and readers understand your message.

Where Should You Use Keywords?

To get the best results, place your keywords thoughtfully in the following areas:

- Page titles and subheadings (H1, H2)
- The first paragraph of your content
- Image file names and alt text (descriptions of the images)
- Web page URLs (for example, www.yoursite.com/seo-basics)
- Meta tags (explained in the next section)

2. Meta Tags: Describing Your Web Page for Search Engines

Meta tags are snippets of code that provide information about your web page to search engines. They don't appear on the actual page but are included in the website's HTML. Two of the most important meta tags are the meta title and the meta description.

Key Meta Tags:

- **Meta title:** The headline that appears on SERPs. It should include the primary keyword and attract attention. The word count is 60, including space and special characters. **Example:** *How to Start a Business with Low Investment | Step-by-Step Guide*
- **Meta description:** A summary that explains what the page is about. It influences whether people click on your link. Words length is 160, including space and special characters. *Example: Learn how to start your own business with a small budget. Follow this beginner-friendly guide with easy steps.*

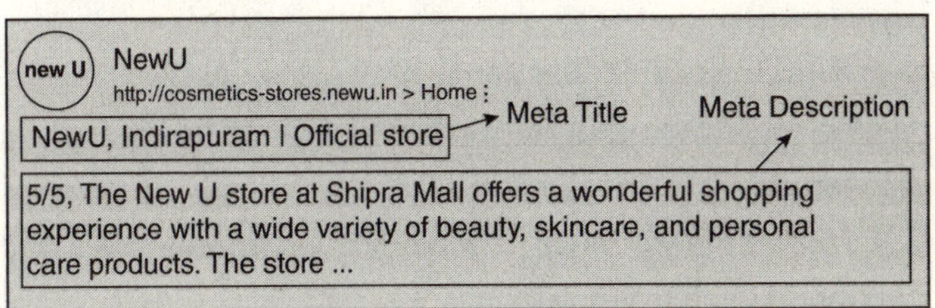

Fig. 4.4: An example of key meta tags

Why Are Meta Tags Useful?

Meta tags are an essential part of on-page SEO because they serve as a website's first impression in search engine results. When users search for information on platforms like Google, the meta title and meta description are usually the first elements they see. These short snippets of text provide a preview of what the page is about and help users decide whether to click on the link. A clear, relevant, and keyword-rich meta title and description increase the likelihood of users clicking on your webpage. This not only improves your click-through rate but also signals to search engines that your content is relevant to the user's query, potentially leading to higher rankings.

According to Yoast (2023), well-written meta tags are directly linked to improved visibility and higher CTRs, especially when they align closely with the search intent of users. Furthermore, Google's SEO Starter Guide (2022) emphasizes that descriptive and keyword-optimized meta tags help both users and search engines better understand the page content.

For example:

- A weak meta title like *Home* or *Welcome to Our Website* gives no meaningful information and may be ignored.
- A strong meta title like *Top 10 Budget Smartphones Under ₹15,000 | 2024 Buying Guide* clearly communicates the content's value and relevance.

Key Benefits of Meta Tags:

- Improve CTR by making your listings more appealing in search results

- Help search engines categorize your content accurately
- Encourage user trust and clicks when titles and descriptions are aligned with what users are searching for
- Allow businesses to highlight key features, benefits, or calls to action before a user even visits the site

3. Backlinks: Earning Trust from Other Websites

We already know what backlinks are. Let's understand them in more detail.

Why Are Backlinks Important?

Backlinks are one of the most influential ranking factors used by search engines like Google. When your website earns backlinks from reputable, high-authority websites, it signals to search engines that your content is trustworthy, relevant, and valuable. This, in turn, increases the likelihood that your pages will rank higher in SERPs.

According to Moz (2024), backlinks continue to be one of the strongest indicators of site authority and influence. In fact, websites that consistently earn high-quality backlinks tend to outrank those with weak or no link profiles, even if both have similar content quality.

How Can You Get Backlinks?

Getting backlinks may seem difficult at first, but there are several easy and ethical ways for beginners to build them. The key is to create valuable content and share it in the right places where people can discover and link to it.

Here are some beginner-friendly methods to earn backlinks:

1. **Write guest posts:** Offer to write articles for reputable blogs or websites in your niche. In return, most websites allow you to include a link back to your website in the author bio or within the content.
   Example: If you run a blog on sustainable living, write a guest article like '5 Everyday Habits for Eco-Friendly Living' for an environmental blog and link to your site in the article.
2. **Share useful content:** Create helpful, original, and shareable content like how-to guides, infographics, lists, or research posts. If others find your content valuable, they may link to it naturally.
   Example: An infographic on 'The Best Indian Herbs for Skin Care' could get shared and linked by health bloggers or Ayurveda websites.
3. **List your site in directories:** Submit your website to trusted online directories such as Google Business Profile, Justdial, Sulekha, Yelp, and Clutch (for service-based businesses). These listings often include a link to your site and boost local SEO.
4. **Collaborate with influencers:** Reach out to bloggers, YouTubers, or social media influencers in your field. Offer them a free product or resource in exchange for a review and a backlink.
5. **Use social media to promote your content:** Even though social media links are not always counted as SEO backlinks, they help increase visibility. As more

people see your content, some may link to it from their websites or blogs.

6. **Join forums and communities:** Be active in industry-related forums such as Quora, Reddit, or niche Facebook groups. Share helpful tips and include a link to your content when it's relevant (not spammy).
7. **Reclaim unlinked mentions:** Sometimes, websites mention your brand name but do not link to you. Use tools like Google Alerts or Ubersuggest to find such mentions and request the site owner to add a link.

> **Insider Note:** Avoid getting backlinks from unrelated, spammy, or low-quality websites. These can harm your website's SEO and reputation.

Free SEO Tools

You do not need to invest in expensive software to start improving your website's search engine ranking. Several free SEO tools offer powerful features that can help you understand your audience, optimize your website, and track your performance on search engines like Google.

Below are two essential and beginner-friendly tools every digital marketer should know.

1. **Google Search Console (GSC):** This is a free tool offered by Google. It helps you monitor and improve how your website appears in Google search results.

   With GSC, you can:

   - See which pages of your website are visible on Google

- Know what keywords people are using to find your site
- Check how many people are clicking on your website from search results
- Find and fix technical problems like broken links or mobile errors

2. **Ubersuggest (by Neil Patel):** Ubersuggest is a beginner-friendly SEO tool that gives you a full overview of your website and keyword performance.

   With Ubersuggest, you can:

   - Do keyword research to find terms people are searching for
   - Check your website's SEO score and performance
   - See what keywords your competitors are using
   - Discover new content ideas based on search data

   > **Insider Note:** Add your website to Google Search Console as soon as it is live. It is easy to use and very helpful for beginners.

   It offers clear, easy-to-understand insights and is great for people just getting started with SEO.

3. **Google Trends:** Google Trends shows you what people are searching for on Google in real time. This tool is very helpful for planning blog posts, YouTube content, or social media campaigns. It helps you stay updated with the latest trends.

   You can use Google Trends to:

   - Identify popular or rising keywords in your niche

- Understand seasonal trends (such as winter skincare tips or Diwali gift ideas)
- Compare two topics or keywords to see which one is more popular

4. **Answer The Public:** This tool helps you find real questions that people ask on search engines. Answer The Public is great for creating blog titles, FAQ sections, or video content that matches user intent. It organizes common search phrases into helpful categories.

   It shows:

   - What people are asking about your keyword
   - Popular 'how', 'what', 'why', and 'when' questions
   - Comparison phrases like 'digital marketing versus traditional marketing'
   - Long-tail keyword ideas for more targeted content

5. **Yoast SEO Plug-In (for WordPress Users):** If your website is built using WordPress, the Yoast SEO plug-in makes it easy to manage your on-page SEO. It is one of the most popular SEO tools for WordPress users and is ideal for beginners who are updating their website content themselves.

   Yoast helps you:

   - Add SEO-friendly page titles and meta descriptions
   - Check keyword usage within your content
   - Improve the readability of your pages and posts
   - Get real-time SEO suggestions while writing

Simple SEO Practices

You do not need to be an expert to improve your website's SEO. By following a few basic and practical steps, you can make your website more visible on search engines and attract more visitors over time.

1. **Choose the right keywords:** Think about the words your audience might type on Google to find your website. Use free tools like Ubersuggest or Google Keyword Planner to discover these keywords. Once you see them, add them naturally to your titles, headings, content, and image descriptions.
2. **Write helpful and clear content:** Your content should answer questions or solve problems for your readers. Use simple language and short paragraphs. Break up the content using subheadings so that it is easy to follow. Well-written content often ranks better in search results.
3. **Use clear titles and meta descriptions:** Every page should have a unique and meaningful title. Also, write a short meta description (about 150 to 160 characters) that summarizes what the page is about. This helps both search engines and readers understand your content.
4. **Add internal links:** Connect your web pages and blog posts by linking them to each other. This helps visitors explore more content on your site and also improves how search engines understand your site's structure.
5. **Use images with alt text:** Images make your website more attractive, but search engines cannot see them. They read the 'alt text' you add to each image. Always

describe your images using short, relevant phrases so they are accessible and appear in image search results.

6. **Make your website mobile-friendly:** Most people browse websites using their mobile phones or tablets. Use a responsive design or mobile-friendly design themes so that your site adjusts well to all screen sizes. A mobile-friendly or responsive site improves the user experience (UX) and is favoured by the Google Search browser.
7. **Update your content regularly:** Websites with fresh and updated content perform better. Review and update old blog posts, fix outdated information, and add new examples or tips. Keeping your content current tells search engines that your website is active and relevant.
8. **Submit your site to Google Search Console:** Use Google Search Console to submit your website and track how it appears in search results. You can also use it to identify and fix issues. It is a free and important tool for improving your website's SEO health.
9. **Focus on website speed:** A slow website can frustrate users and harm your search ranking. To improve speed, compress large images, remove unnecessary plug-ins, and test your site using Google Page Speed Insights. A faster site keeps visitors engaged for longer.

New Trends in SEO

As search engines evolve, so should your SEO knowledge. Here are a few trends beginners should be aware of:

- **Helpful content update:** Google now rewards websites that offer real value. AI-written or copied content may not rank well if it's not useful.
- **Voice search optimization:** People are asking Google questions out loud using phones or smart speakers. Include natural, question-based content like 'How can I start yoga at home?'
- **E-E-A-T (experience, expertise, authoritativeness, trustworthiness):** Google checks if your content is written by someone with real experience. Add your name, a small author bio, and trustworthy sources.
- **Mobile-first indexing:** Your mobile site matters more than your desktop version. Always test how your site looks and works on phones.
- **Core web vitals:** These are speed and user experience metrics that Google considers when ranking your site. Make sure your site loads fast and is easy to use.

Quick Bytes

- SEO helps your website appear in search results without paid ads.
- It includes technical SEO, on-page activities (within the site), and off-page efforts (outside the site).
- Focus on keywords, meta tags, quality content, mobile usability, and backlinks.
- Technical SEO ensures fast loading, mobile-friendliness, and secure browsing.

- On-page SEO improves your content, headings, internal links, and image alt text.
- Off-page SEO builds your site's reputation through backlinks, social shares, and online mentions.
- Use free tools like Google® Search Console, Ubersuggest®, Google Trends and Yoast® SEO.
- Write clear and helpful content using relevant keywords in natural ways.
- Link pages within your site to improve user experience and SEO structure.
- Update content regularly to stay relevant and visible in search engines.

Self-Assessment Questions *(For Revision and Reflection)*

1. When you search for something on Google, why do you think some websites always appear on the first page while others are hidden far behind?
2. If you were running a small business website, what simple steps would you take to make sure more people can find it online?
3. Think about a website you left because it loaded too slowly or was confusing to navigate. How do you think issues like speed and usability affect its ranking on search engines?
4. Imagine you are writing a blog. What kind of title or description would make people want to click on your page in search results?

5. What are some easy but powerful changes you think beginners can make to their website that would help attract more visitors through Google search?

References

1. R. Berman and Z. Katona, 'The Role of Search Engine Optimization in Search Marketing', Marketing Science 39, no. 1 (2020): 132–155.
2. Rand Fishkin, *The Art of SEO: Mastering Search Engine Optimization*, 3rd ed. (Sebastopol, CA: O'Reilly Media, 2015).
3. Google Search Central, *Search Engine Optimization (SEO) Starter Guide* (Google, 2022).
4. HubSpot, *State of Marketing Report* (HubSpot, 2023).
5. Moz, *Beginner's Guide to SEO* (2024), https://moz.com/beginners-guide-to-seo.
6. Yoast, 'How to Craft Effective Meta Descriptions for SEO' (Yoast, 2023).

Chapter 5

Social Media Marketing

Social Media Marketing

Social media marketing (SMM) is the use of digital platforms such as Facebook, Instagram, LinkedIn, YouTube, and X (formerly Twitter) to promote a product, service, or brand. It involves creating and sharing content, including images, videos, captions, and links, to connect with users, build brand awareness, encourage engagement, increase website visits, and boost sales.

Unlike traditional marketing, which focuses on one-way communication through print or television, social media enables two-way interaction. Brands can engage with their audience in real time, respond to feedback, share updates, and strengthen relationships with customers.

According to Statista (2024), the average internet user spends approximately two and a half hours per day on social media. This makes it an essential space for marketers to reach and influence their target audience. SMM helps businesses to

- Reach a large and well-defined audience based on interests, location, or demographics,

- Build trust and customer relationships through consistent engagement,
- Share real-time updates, offers, or announcements quickly and easily,
- Drive traffic to websites and generate leads or direct sales.

Types of Social Media Marketing

There are two main ways to carry out social media marketing:

1. **Organic Social Media:** Organic marketing involves posting free content such as regular updates, stories, and videos and interacting with followers through likes, comments, and shares. It is ideal for building long-term relationships and developing a brand's identity and trust.
2. **Paid Social Media Marketing:** Paid SMM involves investing in advertisements, promoted posts, or sponsored content. These campaigns can be targeted to reach users based on their age, location, interests, or behaviour. Paid methods are especially useful for increasing reach, promoting time-sensitive offers, or retargeting past visitors.

   Example scenario: A small clothing store shares regular updates on Instagram by posting pictures of its new arrivals. They use simple captions such as 'New summer collection just in!' along with hashtags like #SummerStyle and #AffordableFashion. Followers often engage by commenting on the posts, asking about prices, and placing orders through direct messages.

Why Social Media Is Crucial

Social media is no longer just a space for chatting or sharing photos. Today it plays an essential role in people's daily lives. Millions of users spend time on platforms like Facebook, Instagram, YouTube, X, and LinkedIn to stay informed, entertained, and connected. More importantly, people now use these platforms to discover new products, follow brands, watch reviews, and even shop directly from posts.

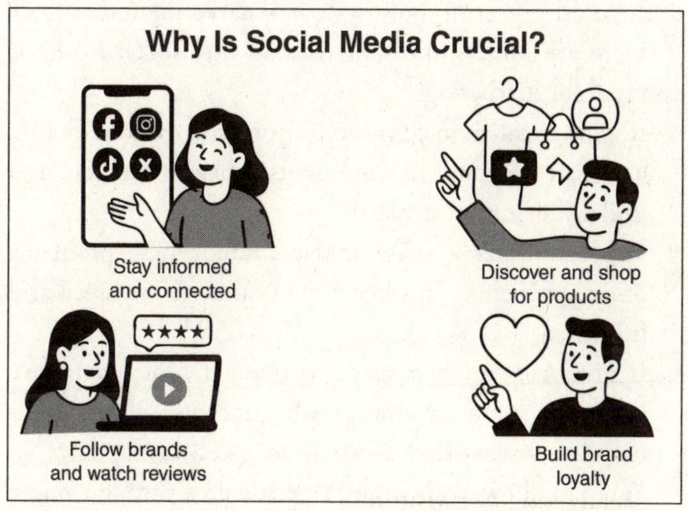

Fig. 5.1: Importance of social media

For businesses of all sizes, this offers a valuable opportunity. You do not need a fancy office or a large marketing budget to succeed. Even a small business or home-based start-up can grow simply by showing up consistently on social media. When people see your brand regularly, they begin to recognize it, trust it, and eventually become loyal customers.

Why Social Media Is Essential in Marketing

Social media has changed how businesses communicate with their customers. It is no longer just a place to advertise. It is a space where you can build relationships, answer questions, and show your brand's personality. According to Hootsuite (2023), more than four billion people around the world use social media, and many of them follow brands to learn about their products and services. This makes social platforms one of the most powerful tools in digital marketing today.

Here are some important reasons why social media is essential for marketing:

- It allows real-time communication with your audience. You can respond to comments, answer queries, and update customers instantly.
- You can quickly share updates about new products, offers, or events. This keeps your audience engaged and informed.
- It gives customers a space to interact. They can leave feedback, share reviews, or ask questions, all of which help improve trust.
- You can show your brand's personality through posts, stories, and videos. This helps people connect with your business on a personal level.
- It helps build a loyal community. By replying to comments, thanking followers, or sharing user content, you create a sense of belonging that encourages repeat engagement.

> **Tip:** You do not need to be on every platform. Start with one or two where your target customers are most active. Be consistent, share useful or interesting content, and respond to comments or messages. Over time, this builds trust and brings real results.

Major Platforms: Facebook, Instagram, LinkedIn, YouTube, X

Each social media platform works in a different way and serves a unique purpose. As a beginner, it is important to understand which platform is best suited for your business or brand. Here is a simple overview of the most popular platforms:

- **Facebook:** Facebook is one of the oldest and most widely used platforms. It is great for building a community, sharing regular updates, and running targeted ads. Local shops, service providers, and family-focused brands often perform well here because it offers strong tools for reaching specific age groups, locations, and interests.
- **Instagram:** Instagram is a visual platform where pictures, short videos, and stories are the focus. It works well for brands in fashion, food, travel, beauty, and lifestyle. Businesses use reels, stories, and product posts to catch attention and grow quickly. It is best for brands that have strong visuals to share.
- **LinkedIn:** LinkedIn is a professional platform used mainly for business networking, job updates, and expert content. It is ideal for B2B (business-to-business) marketing,

personal branding, freelancers, and consultants. If you are offering corporate services, training, or education-related content, LinkedIn helps you connect with professionals.

- **YouTube:** YouTube is the largest video-sharing platform. It is perfect for long videos such as tutorials, how-to guides, reviews, and educational content. YouTube content stays active for a long time and can bring consistent traffic if your videos are helpful. Businesses use it to build trust and explain their products in detail.
- **X:** Formerly Twitter, X is a fast-moving platform used for short messages, updates, trends, and public discussions. It is commonly used by news channels, politicians, public figures, and brands that want to share thoughts, respond to customer queries, or join trending conversations. It works well when your content is short, timely, and relevant.

Creating a Social Media Calendar

Posting content without a clear plan often leads to confusion, inconsistency, and missed opportunities. You may forget important dates, run out of ideas, or end up posting at the wrong time. To stay organized and maintain a regular presence on social media, it is helpful to use a social media calendar. This calendar serves as a clear schedule that outlines what to post, when to post, and on which platform. Whether you are a freelancer, a small business owner, or part of a marketing team, using a content calendar helps you stay focused and avoid last-minute stress.

What Is a Social Media Calendar?

A social media calendar is a planning tool that helps you schedule and organize your posts in advance. It can be as simple as a handwritten planner, an Excel sheet, or a digital tool like Google Calendar, Trello, or Meta Business Suite. According to HubSpot (2024), marketers who use content calendars are 60 per cent more likely to publish consistently and report higher audience engagement over time.

It allows you to

- Stay consistent with your posting schedule,
- Align content with business goals, product launches, or festivals,
- Plan for promotions, sales, or awareness campaigns,
- Save time by preparing content in batches,
- Maintain a balance of different content types (such as tips, testimonials, product updates, and reels).

Example of a Simple Weekly Calendar

Day	Post Idea
Monday	Motivational quote or tip
Wednesday	Product feature or behind-the-scenes photo
Friday	Customer testimonial or review
Sunday	Fun poll, quiz, or short reel

Tools to Create a Calendar

You do not need expensive software to create and manage a social media calendar. Many beginners start with a simple Excel spreadsheet or Google Sheet, which can be easily customized to suit your needs. These tools allow you to plan your posts by date, platform, content type, caption ideas, media requirements, and posting time, all in one place.

For those who prefer a more visual or automated experience, several free tools are also available:

- **Buffer:** A user-friendly platform that allows you to schedule posts across different social media accounts. It offers a simple dashboard where you can draft, preview, and publish content at the best times.
- **Canva Content Planner:** Integrated into Canva's free design platform, this tool helps you schedule and manage posts visually. You can design your content in Canva and set a future publishing date, all without leaving the platform.

> **Tip:** Begin with just two or three posts per week and gradually increase your pace as you gain confidence. The key is to stay consistently accurate and accurately consistent. Quality and regularity matter more than quantity.

Fundamentals of Paid Promotions

Posting content on social media without spending money is called organic marketing. It helps build trust, develop relationships, and maintain a brand presence over time. However, organic reach is often limited. Social media platforms such as Facebook and Instagram typically show unpaid posts to only a small percentage of your followers.

For example, if you have a thousand followers, only around two hundred people may see your content in their feed unless they actively engage with your posts.

This decline in organic reach is due to changes in platform algorithms that prioritize content from friends and paid advertisers. As a result, businesses that rely only on organic posting may struggle to grow or reach new audiences. To overcome this challenge and accelerate visibility, many brands use paid promotions. These are advertisements that you pay for, allowing your content to appear in front of a larger and more targeted audience. Paid promotions help you reach people beyond your existing followers and are especially useful for promoting new products, driving website traffic, or running time-sensitive campaigns.

What Are Paid Promotions?

Paid promotions refer to a type of online advertising where you set a budget and decide exactly who should see your content. Unlike organic posts, which rely on platform algorithms and natural engagement, paid promotions allow you to directly target your ideal audience based on specific factors such as age, location, interests, job roles, or online behaviour. You have full control over how much to spend, who will see the ad, when it will appear, and how long it will run. This makes paid promotions highly flexible and efficient, especially for businesses that want faster results or need to promote time-sensitive offers. Paid promotions are particularly useful for businesses that are launching a new product, hosting a sale, or want to increase traffic to their website or social media page.

Example scenario: Imagine you run a small bakery in Jaipur. You want to promote your new range of birthday cakes. With just ₹500, you can create a paid advertisement on Facebook and Instagram. You can choose to show the ad only to people between the ages of 18 and 40 who live within 5 km of your shop and who have an interest in desserts or baked goods.

This means your message will be shown only to those who are more likely to become your customers. It reduces unnecessary spending and increases the chances of meaningful results.

Why Paid Promotions Are Useful

- **Targeting:** You can choose who sees your ads based on age, location, interests, behaviour, or even past website visits.
- **Scalability:** Paid ads allow you to reach thousands of potential customers quickly, depending on your budget.
- **Flexibility:** You can run different types of ads, such as image posts, videos, stories, or carousels, depending on your goal.
- **Performance tracking**: Platforms like Meta Ads Manager or LinkedIn Campaign Manager provide detailed analytics, so you can monitor how your ad is performing and adjust it as needed.

Did you know? According to the DataReportal Global Digital Report (2024), social media advertising reached more than 4.7 billion users worldwide, making it one of the most cost-effective and scalable tools for digital marketers.

Beginner-Friendly Tools to Help You Run and Manage Paid Promotions

There are several free and beginner-friendly tools that help you plan, design, run, and track your ads more easily. Here are the most used tools for social media marketing.

1. **Meta Business Suite:** It is a free and user-friendly tool provided by Meta, the parent company of Facebook and Instagram.

   What you can do with Meta Business Suite:

   - **Unified dashboard:** Manage your Facebook and Instagram accounts together from a single dashboard.
   - **Post scheduling:** Plan and schedule posts, stories, and reels in advance for both platforms.
   - **Messaging:** Respond to messages and comments from Facebook and Instagram in one inbox.
   - **Insights and analytics:** Track the performance of your posts, measure audience engagement, and monitor page growth through detailed metrics.
   - **Ad management:** Create and manage simple ads to promote posts, boost page visibility, or reach new audiences.

- **Content planning:** View your scheduled posts in calendar format to keep your content organized and consistent.

2. **Canva:** It is a free online graphic design tool that is perfect for creating attractive and professional-looking content, even if you have no background in design. It is widely used by students, freelancers, small businesses, and social media managers to produce high-quality visuals for digital platforms. Canva can be accessed through your computer browser or mobile app, and it offers a variety of design formats suited for social media, presentations, posters, videos, banners, and more.

   Why you will love Canva:

   - **Templates:** Canva provides thousands of ready-made templates for Instagram posts, Facebook covers, YouTube thumbnails, story slides, and more.
   - **Easy editing:** The drag-and-drop interface allows you to customize templates by changing text, colours, images, and fonts.
   - **Free media library**: You can use a wide selection of free photos, illustrations, icons, stickers, and fonts to make your designs stand out.
   - **Content planner:** Canva includes a scheduling feature that lets you design and plan your social media posts in advance for platforms like Facebook and Instagram.
   - **Team collaboration:** You can invite team members to view or edit your designs, making it easy to work together on projects.

- **No design skills needed:** Its simple tools and clean interface allow even first-time users to create professional-looking content in minutes.

3. **Creator Studio:** Creator Studio is a free content management tool provided by Meta. It is designed to help individuals and businesses manage their Facebook and Instagram pages, with a strong focus on video content. While it shares some features with Meta Business Suite, Creator Studio is especially useful for content creators, video publishers, and marketers who regularly post and manage video-based content. This tool can be accessed from a web browser and is ideal for those who want to track content performance, monetize videos, and organize large volumes of posts more effectively.

With Creator Studio, you can do these:

- **Video publishing and scheduling:** Upload and schedule videos to Facebook and Instagram directly from one dashboard.
- **Performance insights:** Monitor views, audience retention, engagement, and reach for each video post.
- **Monetization tools:** Eligible creators can earn revenue through ads placed in videos using the in-stream ads feature.
- **Content library:** View, manage, and filter all your past posts, videos, and drafts in one organized place.
- **Inbox management:** Read and reply to comments and messages from both platforms in a centralized inbox.

- **Multi-page management:** Manage multiple Facebook pages without logging in and out.

> **Tip:** Start with a small ad campaign for three or five days. Choose one clear goal, such as getting more profile visits, increasing WhatsApp messages, or gaining new followers. Once the campaign is complete, check the results and improve the next campaign based on what worked best.

Types of Ads You Can Run on Social Media

When you decide to promote your business on social media, it is important to choose the right type of ad based on your goal. Each ad type serves a different purpose, such as increasing brand awareness, getting more messages, or driving traffic to your website. Most platforms like Facebook, Instagram, and LinkedIn allow you to choose from these common types:

1. **Image ads:** Image ads are one of the simplest and most widely used types of social media advertisements. They consist of a single image accompanied by a caption, a headline, and a call to action (CTA) button such as 'Shop Now', 'Learn More', or 'Sign Up'. These ads are ideal for highlighting a product, service, offer, or event in a visually appealing way. Because of their straightforward format, they are easy to create and work well on platforms like Facebook, Instagram, and LinkedIn. To be effective, the image should be high quality, relevant to the message,

and attention grabbing. The accompanying text should be short and clear and encourage the viewer to take the next step.

Image ads are especially useful when you want to

- Showcase a specific product or collection,
- Promote a seasonal discount or announcement,
- Raise brand awareness with clear visuals.

2. **Video ads:** Video ads use moving visuals to promote a product, service, or idea. They allow businesses to show their offerings in action, explain features, or tell stories that connect with the audience. Compared to image ads, videos are more dynamic and often more engaging. These ads can be short clips of around 15 to 30 seconds or longer, depending on the platform. Popular social media platforms like Facebook, Instagram, YouTube, and LinkedIn support video ads in different formats like feed videos, stories, or promotional videos that play before or during other content. A good video ad should be clear, visually attractive, and deliver its main message in the first few seconds. Adding captions can make the message more accessible, especially for users who watch without sound.

   Video ads are useful for

   - demonstrating how a product works,
   - telling a story that builds interest or emotion,
   - grabbing attention through sound and movement,
   - increasing shares and user engagement.

Fig. 5.2: How a Facebook carousel looks like

3. **Carousel ads:** These ads allow you to showcase multiple images or videos within a single ad, arranged in a swipeable format. Each slide in the carousel can have its own headline, description, and clickable link, giving you the flexibility to highlight different products, features, or steps in a process.

   Carousel ads are commonly used on platforms like Facebook, Instagram, and LinkedIn. (It is also common on Amazon.) They help increase engagement because users spend more time exploring each part of the ad. The interactive nature of the format also makes it easier to guide viewers towards specific actions or landing pages. To make carousel ads effective, use high-quality visuals, keep the messaging consistent across slides, and ensure that each card offers something valuable to the viewer.

This format is effective for

- displaying a range of products in one ad,
- telling a step-by-step brand or product story,
- comparing features or offers side by side,
- encouraging users to interact by swiping through the cards.

4. **Story ads:** These ads are short, full-screen vertical advertisements that appear between user stories on platforms like Instagram and Facebook. They are designed to be quick, visually engaging, and mobile friendly. They usually last for just a few seconds and disappear after 24 hours, unless the viewer acts or the brand saves them as highlights.

   Story ads blend naturally into a user's viewing experience and often include interactive elements such as swipe-up links, polls, stickers, or call-to-action buttons like 'Shop Now' or 'Learn More'. To get the most out of story ads, use strong visuals, keep the message short and clear, and include a clear call to action that encourages viewers to take the next step.

   They are effective for

   - promoting limited-time offers or flash sales,
   - sharing quick updates or behind-the-scenes content,
   - driving direct traffic to product pages or websites,
   - reaching mobile users in an immersive and engaging way.

5. **Message ads (click-to-direct message):** Message ads are a type of advertisement designed to start a direct conversation between the business and the customer. When a user clicks on the ad, it opens a messaging app such as WhatsApp, Facebook Messenger, or Instagram Direct, allowing them to chat instantly with the brand.

Fig. 5.3: An example of a message ad

Message ads work well for businesses that want to offer a more personalized experience or handle customer queries quickly. They are also popular with small businesses that manage customer communication directly through mobile phones. To make message ads effective, include a clear and inviting call to action such as 'Chat with us', 'Ask a question', or 'Send a message'. Also, be prepared to respond quickly as users expect real-time replies in messaging platforms.

These ads are useful for

- answering product or service-related questions in real time,
- providing personal support or guidance before a purchase,
- collecting leads or taking orders directly through chat,
- building relationships through one-on-one interaction.

6. **Website traffic ads:** Website traffic ads are designed to direct users from social media platforms to a specific page on your website. This could be a blog post, product detail page, sign-up form, contact page, or any other landing page you want to promote.

Fig. 5.4: An example of a website traffic ad

These ads include a strong call to action, such as 'Visit Now', 'Learn More', or 'Shop Now', and typically appear on platforms like Facebook, Instagram, LinkedIn, and X. When a user clicks the ad, they are taken directly to the selected web page. To make these ads effective, use a clear image or video, a short but strong message, and ensure the web page loads quickly and is mobile friendly. The success of a traffic ad depends not only on the ad itself but also on the quality and relevance of the webpage where the user is directed.

Website traffic ads are useful for

- driving visitors to your blog, store, or service pages,
- promoting new product launches or seasonal offers,
- collecting leads through forms or sign-up pages,
- increasing overall website engagement and reach.

7. **Lead generation ads:** Lead generation ads are a type of advertisement that helps businesses collect contact information, such as names, email addresses, or phone numbers, directly within the social media platform. These ads use a form that opens inside the app itself, so users do not need to leave the platform to share their details.

   For example, on Facebook or Instagram, when someone clicks a lead generation ad, a form appears with their basic details already filled in. This makes it easy and quick for users to sign up or show interest, increasing the chances of getting more responses. If your goal is to get more people to message you, start with click-to-message ads. If you want more website visits, try traffic ads. Always test, learn, and improve with each campaign. To make lead generation ads successful, it is important to keep the form short and offer clear value to the user. Following up quickly also improves trust and conversion rates.

Fig. 5.5: An example of a lead generation ad

These ads are useful for

- getting sign-ups for newsletters, offers, or events,
- collecting inquiries for products or services,
- building a list of potential customers for follow-up,
- offering something in return, such as a free trial, guide, or discount.

Cost Comparison of Popular Social Media Marketing Services

Different social media marketing services come with different cost levels. Even though exact prices keep changing based on platform policies and agency charges, businesses should understand which services are generally lower-cost, moderately priced, and higher-cost. This helps in planning a realistic marketing budget.

Cost Level	Service Type	General Nature
Lower Cost	Organic posting	No ad spend required, regular content and engagement
Lower Cost	Boosted post	Small budget, paid reach to a limited audience
Moderate Cost	Facebook and Instagram Ads	Targeting-based campaigns for leads, traffic, or sales
Moderate–High Cost	Google Search ads	High-intent traffic but high competition in many industries
High Cost	Influencer marketing	Depends on influencer popularity and audience size
High Cost	YouTube video ads	Professional video creation + ad placement budget

Which service is suitable for which type of business?

Type of Business	Recommended Service	Reason
A new bakery in a local market	Organic posting + boosted posts	Budget-friendly, helps brand visibility in nearby localities

A preschool or coaching institute	Facebook and Instagram lead ads	Parents/students actively search for education-related services online
An online store selling gifts or jewellery	Meta conversion ads + influencer marketing	Higher return on investment (ROI) through impulse purchases + trust through influencer
A real estate company	Google Search ads	People actively search for 'flat for sale', 'property near me', etc.
A mobile app-based start-up	YouTube ads	Video storytelling builds strong recall for new tech products
A well-known beauty or fashion brand	Influencer marketing + Reels ads	Visual content + social proof drives high engagement and conversions

Quick Bytes

- SMM uses platforms like Facebook, Instagram, LinkedIn, YouTube, and X to promote products, services, or personal brands.
- It helps you reach your target audience, build trust, and grow your business through both organic content and paid promotions.
- Even small businesses or home-based sellers can succeed on social media with consistent posting and simple visuals.

- A social media calendar keeps your content organized, timely, and varied, helping you plan ahead for festivals, offers, or campaigns.
- Paid ads help you reach a wider and more specific audience, even with a small budget, and provide measurable results like clicks, leads, or sales.
- Common ad types include image ads, video ads, carousel ads, story ads, click-to-message ads, website traffic ads, and lead generation ads.
- Tools like Meta Business Suite, Canva, and Creator Studio make it easier to create, schedule, and manage content and ad campaigns.
- Choosing the right ad type depends on your goal, such as increasing sales, gaining followers, or collecting leads.

Self-Assessment Questions *(For Revision and Reflection)*

1. How has social media changed the way people discover and trust brands today?
2. Imagine you are launching a new café in your city. How would you use Instagram or Facebook to attract your first one hundred customers?
3. Why are paid ads considered more effective than organic posts for reaching a targeted audience on social media?
4. Which social media marketing service would you prioritize for a small business with a limited budget, and why?
5. Do you believe a small business can grow only through organic posts, or are paid promotions also important? Share your thoughts.

References

1. Hootsuite, *The Global State of Digital 2023* (Vancouver: Hootsuite, 2023).
2. HubSpot, 'How to Create a Social Media Content Calendar: Tips and Free Templates', 2024.
3. Statista, 'Average Daily Social Media Usage Worldwide', 2024.

Chapter 6

The Essentials of Running Paid Campaigns on Google and Meta

What Is Paid Advertising?

Paid digital advertising allows businesses to appear instantly in front of potential customers who are actively searching for something or are likely to be interested, based on their online behaviour and preferences. Two of the most widely used platforms for paid digital advertising are:

- **Google Ads**, which include search ads, YouTube ads, and display ads
- **Meta Ads**, which include advertisements on Facebook and Instagram

These platforms are powerful because they give you control over who sees your ads, when they see them, and what message or promotion they receive. You do not need a large marketing team or a big budget to get started. Even a small local business can run effective campaigns by selecting the right platform and targeting options.

In simple terms, paid advertising in digital marketing means paying a platform like Google or Meta to promote your product, service, or brand to a chosen audience. This approach is different from organic marketing, where you post content and rely on people to discover it naturally. Paid ads deliver faster visibility and results, making them especially useful when launching a new product, running a limited-time offer, or entering a competitive market (Kotler et al. 2021).

Example scenario: A new café in Mumbai runs a Meta ad campaign targeting people aged 20 to 40 who live within 3 km of its location and are interested in coffee or desserts. The campaign promotes a 'Buy One Get One Free' offer for the opening week. Within three days, the café attracts over 500 new customers, many of whom become repeat visitors.

Why Use Paid Ads?

- **Faster results:** Paid ads appear immediately to the selected audience.
- **Precise targeting:** You can choose who sees the ad based on age, gender, location, interests, online activity, and more.
- **Budget control:** You can decide how much you want to spend per day or per campaign.
- **Measurable outcomes:** You can track how many people saw the ad, clicked it, visited your website, or took any other action.

Common Payment Models in Paid Advertising

1. **Pay-per-click (PPC):** You are charged only when someone clicks on your ad. This is common in Google search ads.

2. **Cost-per-mille (CPM):** You are charged for every one thousand impressions (views). This model is often used in display or video ads.
3. **Cost-per-view (CPV):** You are charged when someone watches your video ad, used especially in YouTube campaigns.
4. **Cost-per-action (CPA):** You are charged only when someone takes a specific action, like signing up or purchasing.

Example Scenario: Google Search Ad for a Coaching Institute

A coaching institute in Delhi wants to promote its online crash course for NEET aspirants. They run a Google Search ad with the keyword 'best NEET coaching online'. Now, whenever a student or parent types this phrase on Google, the ad appears at the top of the search results. The ad includes a short message like 'Join our 30-Day Crash Course – 100% Online. Limited Seats!' and a link to the registration page. The institute pays only when someone clicks on the ad, which helps them control their budget while reaching students who are actively looking for help.

Google Ads: Google Ads, formerly known as Google AdWords, is an online advertising platform developed by Google that allows businesses to display advertisements to people who are actively searching for products, services, or information online. These ads appear across Google Search, YouTube, Gmail, and millions of partner websites within the Google Display Network. When a user types a query on Google, such as *best yoga classes near me*, relevant ads appear at the top of the search results page. These are clearly marked as 'Sponsored' and are highly effective because they target users who already have an interest in the topic.

Google Ads primarily operates on a pay-per-click (PPC) model, which means advertisers only pay when someone clicks on their ad. This ensures that marketing budgets are spent on engaged prospects rather than passive viewers. Businesses can customize their campaigns by selecting a target audience, location, keywords, and budget, making Google Ads a flexible and scalable option for organizations of all sizes. Google Ads is effective for increasing brand visibility, driving website traffic, generating more calls or messages, and boosting online sales. With careful keyword selection, budget optimization, and proper tracking, even small campaigns can deliver significant returns on investment (Berman and Katona 2013).

Main Types of Google Ads:

- **Search ads:** Text-based ads that appear in Google Search results when users look for relevant terms.

  Real example: Urban Company® runs search ads targeting keywords such as 'home cleaning services near me' or 'salon at home', ensuring their ads show up at the top when users actively search for these services.

- **Display ads:** Image or banner ads shown on partner websites and apps within the Google Display Network.

  Real example: Lenskart® regularly uses display ads featuring discount offers and new arrivals to retarget users who previously visited its website.

- **Video ads:** Short promotional videos shown before or during YouTube content.

  Real example: Zomato® ran short humorous video ads on YouTube promoting food delivery during cricket events and festive seasons.

- **Shopping ads:** Product-focused ads showing images, prices, and store names, mostly used by e-commerce brands.

  Real example: Myntra® and Croma® use Google shopping ads to show product pictures, discounts, and ratings directly in search results for queries like 'women's heels' or 'best smart TV'.

- **App promotion ads:** Ads encouraging users to download or engage with a mobile application.

  Real example: Meesho® uses app promotion ads to target small business owners and shoppers, encouraging them to download the app with taglines like 'Start your online business from home—no investment'.

Meta Ads: Meta Ads refer to paid advertising campaigns run across platforms owned by Meta, including Facebook, Instagram, and Messenger. These ads enable businesses to reach audiences based on interests, behaviours, demographics, and previous online interactions. Unlike Google Ads, which target people actively searching for information, Meta Ads reach users while they are browsing, scrolling, or engaging with content on social media.

Meta Ads are designed to be highly visual, often incorporating high-quality images, brand colours, and consistent fonts to capture attention and build trust instantly. They can appear in different formats, such as single image ads, video ads, carousel ads, or stories. Advertisers can select from a range of campaign objectives, including driving website visits, increasing followers, generating more messages, or directly promoting a product or service (Chaffey and Ellis-Chadwick 2022).

Audience Targeting in Meta Ads

One of the strongest features of Meta Ads is its detailed audience targeting system. Advertisers can customize their audience using parameters such as:

- Location (for example, people living in Delhi)
- Age and gender
- Interests (such as fashion, fitness, or education)
- Behaviours (such as frequent travellers or online shoppers)
- Custom audiences (such as users who visited your website or engaged with your content)

Meta Ads operate on either a pay-per-click or a cost-per-impression model. In PPC, advertisers pay only when someone clicks on the ad, while in CPM, payment is based on the number of times the ad is shown. This flexibility allows businesses of all sizes to optimize their campaigns according to specific goals and budgets (Tuten and Solomon 2020). Meta also provides integrated tools, such as Meta Business Suite, which allows advertisers to create ads, schedule organic posts, and monitor performance metrics in one place. Meta Ads are particularly effective for building brand awareness, generating leads, and encouraging engagement among audiences who may not be actively searching but are likely to be interested in your offering.

Example scenario: Suppose you are launching an online course for students. You could run a Facebook and Instagram ad targeting people aged 18 to 24 who live in your city and are interested in education or competitive exams. The ad might feature a visually appealing brochure of the course with a call to action, such as *Send Message*, allowing interested students to contact you directly via Instagram or Facebook Messenger.

Google Ads vs Facebook (Meta) Ads: A Simple Comparison

When it comes to running paid campaigns online, both Google Ads and Meta Ads (Facebook and Instagram) offer powerful tools. However, they work in different ways and serve different purposes. Understanding these differences can help you choose the right platform based on your business goals.

Feature	Google Ads	Meta (Facebook and Instagram) Ads
Ad Platform Type	Intent-based (people actively searching)	Interest-based (people browsing and scrolling)
Where Ads Appear	Google Search, YouTube, websites, mobile apps	Facebook, Instagram, Messenger, Audience network
Best For	Capturing leads, sales, or traffic from users who are searching with intent	Building brand awareness, engagement, visual storytelling, and lead generation

Targeting Method	Keywords, location, device, time, audience types	Demographics, interests, behaviours, custom audiences
Ad Formats	Text ads (search), display banners, shopping ads, video ads (YouTube)	Image ads, video ads, carousel ads, story ads, click-to-message ads
User Mindset	High intent – users are looking for a solution	Casual browsing – users are open to discovery
Cost	Can be more expensive for high-demand keywords	Generally lower cost per clicks or impression
Speed of Results	Quick, especially for search ads	Quick, especially for awareness or engagement campaigns
Visual Appeal	Less visual (except YouTube and Display)	Highly visual (images, reels, videos, stories)

Google vs Meta: When to Use What

Both Google Ads and Meta Ads are powerful advertising platforms, but they serve slightly different purposes. Understanding when to use each can help you get better results based on your business goals.

Use Google Ads when

- People are actively searching for your product or service (it is perfect for intent-driven results like online shopping, lead generation, or service bookings),
- You want to appear at the exact moment someone types relevant keywords into Google (e.g., 'best coaching for NEET in Delhi'),

- You offer services or products that solve immediate problems or fulfil direct needs.

Why: Google Ads work on 'search intent', meaning the user is already looking for something, and your ad provides the solution.

Use Meta Ads when

- You want to increase brand awareness, promote offers, or connect with people based on their interests and lifestyles.
- Our audience is not actively searching but might be interested if they discover your brand while browsing social media.
- You want to build brand awareness, reach a broad audience, or engage users visually. It is great for storytelling, community building, and promoting offers through eye-catching content.

Why: Meta Ads are more about 'discovery and interest'. You can build relationships, educate your audience, and stay visible with engaging content.

> **Insider Note:** If you have a limited budget, start with Meta Ads because they are more affordable and offer a good learning experience. Once you're comfortable and want to reach users who are actively searching, explore Google Ads as well.

Budgeting and Tracking Results

One of the biggest advantages of advertising on Google or Meta is the flexibility to start small and scale as you see success. You do not need a massive budget to begin. In fact, both platforms allow you to start with as little as ₹100 per day, making paid advertising accessible even for small businesses and start-ups. You can set either a daily budget, which limits how much you spend per day, or a lifetime budget, which spreads your spending over the entire campaign duration.

Key Metrics to Track

Once your ad is live, both Google and Meta offer powerful reporting dashboards that show exactly how your campaigns are performing. Some of the most important metrics include:

- **Impressions:** The number of times your ad appears on a user's screen.
- **Clicks and click-through-rate:** The total clicks your ad receives and the percentage of viewers who clicked on it. A higher CTR often means your ad is relevant and engaging.
- **Cost-per-click:** The average amount you pay for each click. This helps evaluate the efficiency of your spending.
- **Conversions:** The number of people who completed a desired action after clicking your ad, such as filling out a form, calling your business, making a purchase, or downloading a brochure.

Where to Monitor Your Results

- **Google Ads Manager:** Provides detailed insights into keywords, audience locations, devices, and conversions.

- **Meta Ads Manager:** Tracks Facebook and Instagram ads, showing performance by age, interest, region, and other audience segments.

Why Tracking Is Essential

Research shows that advertisers who actively track and adjust campaigns see significantly higher returns on investment compared to those who set and forget their ads (Chaffey 2022).

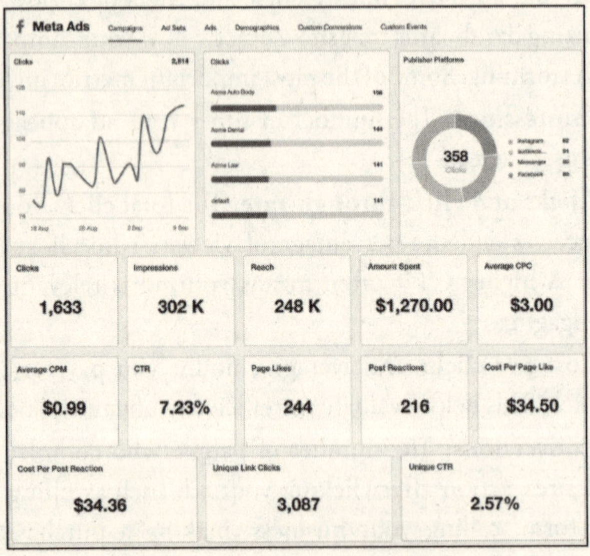

Fig. 6.1: Tracking of an ad performance

Consistently monitoring ad performance allows you to:

- **Identify what is working:** Find the best-performing ads, images, keywords, or audiences.

- **Pause underperforming ads:** Stop ads that are not generating clicks or conversions.
- **Increase spending on winners:** Allocate more budget to ads delivering strong results.
- **Test and optimize:** Experiment with different headlines, visuals, or targeting to continually improve campaign performance.

Visual Campaign Checklist

Question	Example
What is my goal?	Get 100 website visits in 7 days
Who is my target audience?	Students aged 18–25 in Delhi
What content will I use?	A short video with testimonials
What is my budget?	₹1,000 for 5 days
How will I measure success?	Clicks, messages, or downloads

Steps to Create a Google Ad Campaign

Google Ads allow your business to appear on Google Search, YouTube, and partner websites, reaching users who are actively searching for information or browsing related content. Below is a simplified guide to creating a basic Google Search or YouTube ad, suitable for beginners but following best practices recommended by industry experts (Google 2024).

1. **Create a Google Ads Account:** Visit ads.google.com and sign in using your Gmail account. Set your billing country, time zone, and currency. These settings are

important because they determine how you are billed and when your ads are shown.

2. **Choose Your Campaign Goal:** Select what you want to achieve. These are some common goals:
    - Increasing website visits
    - Receiving more phone calls
    - Driving visits to a physical store
    - Promoting a YouTube video
3. **Select Campaign Type:** Decide on the format for your ad. Here's a list of the most popular types:
    - **Search ads:** Text-based ads that appear in Google Search results
    - **Display ads:** Visual banner ads that show on Google's partner websites
    - **Video ads:** Short- or long-form ads that play on YouTube
    - **App promotion ads:** Designed to increase app downloads or engagement
4. **Set Your Target Audience:** Targeting ensures that your ad reaches the right people at the right time (Fishkin 2023). You can narrow your audience based on these factors:
    - **Location:** City, state, or country
    - **Language:** The language your audience speaks
    - **Keywords:** Search terms your audience uses
    - **Device type:** Mobile or desktop devices
5. **Set Budget and Bidding:** Choose how much you want to spend daily or for the entire campaign. Google also lets you select how you will be charged, such as CPC or

CPM. Setting a modest budget initially allows you to test performance before scaling.

6. **Create Your Ad:** Write a clear and engaging headline, followed by a descriptive message. If creating a YouTube ad, upload the video from your channel. Add a call-to-action, such as a website link, phone number, or sign-up button.
7. **Review and Launch:** Double-check your settings, budget, targeting, and ad content. Once everything looks correct, submit your ad for review. In most cases, Google approves ads within a few hours, though this can take up to 24 hours.

Steps to Create a Meta Ad Campaign (Facebook and Instagram)

Meta Ads are created and managed through Meta Ads Manager, which works for both Facebook and Instagram. These ads allow you to connect with highly targeted audiences based on location, interests, demographics, and behaviours. Since Facebook and Instagram have over three billion active users combined, running ads on these platforms provides a significant opportunity for businesses of all sizes (DataReportal 2024).

1. **Create a Meta Business Account:** Visit business.facebook.com and set up your Business Manager account. This acts as the control hub for your advertising. Link your Facebook Page and Instagram account so that you can run ads across both platforms from one dashboard.

2. **Open Meta Ads Manager:** Access adsmanager.facebook.com to create, run, and manage campaigns. Meta Ads Manager offers detailed targeting, budgeting, and reporting tools, which are essential for effective ad performance monitoring.
3. **Select Your Campaign Objective:** Choosing the right objective helps Meta's algorithm optimize ad delivery to people most likely to take your desired action. Choose the goal you want your campaign to achieve. Popular objectives include:
   - Increasing website traffic
   - Getting more messages through WhatsApp or Messenger
   - Boosting engagement, such as likes, shares, and comments
   - Collecting leads through in-platform forms
4. **Define Your Audience:** Precise audience targeting improves ad relevance and cost efficiency (Kotler et al. 2021). You can either create a new audience or use a saved one. Targeting options include:
   - **Location:** Select by city, state, or a radius around a specific point
   - **Age and gender:** Match your demographic profile
   - **Interests:** Such as fitness, travel, technology, or fashion.
   - **Behaviour:** Including frequent online shoppers, travellers, or mobile app users
5. **Set Budget and Duration:** Enter your budget, either per day or for the full campaign duration. Also, choose

the start and end dates. Starting with a small budget allows you to test and optimize your campaign before scaling.

6. **Create Your Ad:** Upload your visuals, write an engaging caption, add a strong headline, and select a call-to-action button, such as 'Learn More', 'Send Message', or 'Shop Now'. Select your ad format based on the type of content you want to showcase:
   - **Single Image or Video:** Great for highlighting one product or offer
   - **Carousel:** Multiple images or videos in a swipeable format
   - **Stories:** Full-screen content for short-term engagement.
   - **Reels:** Short vertical videos with high engagement potential.
   - **Collection:** A mix of images and videos that open into an instant experience.
7. **Choose Placement:** You can allow Meta to automatically place your ad across Facebook, Instagram, Messenger, and Audience Network, or manually select placements. Automatic placements often result in lower costs and broader reach (Meta 2024).
8. **Review and Publish:** Double-check all settings, including your audience, budget, and creative content. Once you are satisfied, click 'Publish'. Meta usually reviews ads within 24 hours. If approved, your ads will start running, and results will appear in Ads Manager.

Quick Bytes

- You don't need to be a digital marketing expert to get started. With basic knowledge and step-by-step guidance, anyone can run effective paid campaigns.
- Paid advertising helps your business appear in front of the right audience quickly, using platforms like Google (Search, YouTube) and Meta (Facebook, Instagram).
- Google Ads are best when people are actively searching for something, while Meta Ads work well for increasing brand awareness and engaging users through visuals.
- Both platforms allow you to start with a small budget, set daily or lifetime limits, and adjust spending based on performance.
- Dashboards like Google Ads Manager and Meta Ads Manager help track impressions, clicks, conversions, and costs, making it easier to improve results over time.
- Even small businesses, tutors, and freelancers can grow their reach and attract customers through simple paid campaigns.

Self-Assessment Questions *(For Revision and Reflection)*

1. Why do you think businesses spend money on online ads when they can post content for free on social media?
2. If you had to promote a new online course, would you choose Google Ads or Meta Ads? What factors would guide your choice?

3. How would you decide the right budget for your first paid campaign as a small business owner?
4. What kind of results would convince you that your ad campaign is performing well?

Which payment model charges an advertiser only when someone clicks on the ad?

References

1. R. Berman and Z. Katona, 'The Role of Search Engine Optimization in Search Marketing', *Marketing Science* 32, no. 4 (2013): 644–651.
2. Dave Chaffey and Fiona Ellis-Chadwick, *Digital Marketing: Strategy, Implementation and Practice*, 8th ed. (Harlow: Pearson, 2022).
3. DataReportal, *Global Digital Overview* (2024).
4. Rand Fishkin, *The Art of SEO: Mastering Search Engine Optimization* (Sebastopol, CA: O'Reilly Media, 2023).
5. Google, *Google Ads Help* (2024).
6. Philip Kotler, Hermawan Kartajaya, and Iwan Setiawan, *Marketing 5.0: Technology for Humanity* (Hoboken, NJ: Wiley, 2021).
7. Meta, *About Meta Ads* (2024).
8. Tracy L. Tuten and Michael R. Solomon, *Social Media Marketing*, 4th ed. (Los Angeles: SAGE Publications, 2020).

Chapter 7

Influencer Marketing

What Is Influencer Marketing?

Influencer marketing is a form of digital marketing where a business partners with individuals who have a loyal and engaged following on social media platforms. These individuals, known as influencers, use their credibility and reach to create and share content that promotes a product, service, or brand in an authentic and relatable manner. Instead of the brand directly advertising itself, the message is delivered through a voice the audience already knows and trusts.

This strategy works effectively because audiences tend to value recommendations from people they admire, often more than from traditional advertising sources. According to Nielsen (2021), 92 per cent of consumers trust recommendations from individuals over brand messages, highlighting the unique power of influencers in shaping consumer decisions. Unlike traditional ads, which often feel intrusive or sales-driven, influencer marketing creates the impression of friendly advice when integrated naturally into the influencer's usual style of content.

Influencer marketing is not limited to large global brands. Even small businesses can benefit from collaborating with local or micro-influencers. Micro-influencers, who may have between 10,000 and 50,000 followers, often enjoy stronger community trust and higher engagement rates compared to mega-influencers. This makes them valuable partners for businesses aiming to reach niche audiences or build brand awareness on a limited budget.

For instance, if a popular fitness coach on Instagram posts about a protein shake they genuinely use after workouts, followers are more likely to trust this recommendation since it aligns with the influencer's expertise and lifestyle. This form of promotion feels genuine and is highly targeted because the product matches the audience's interests.

In short, influencer marketing is especially effective for these purposes:

- Building brand awareness
- Reaching niche and highly engaged audiences
- Driving higher engagement and conversions compared to many traditional advertising methods.

Types of Influencers

Influencers are often grouped into categories based on the number of followers they have. Each type has its own advantages, depending on the goals and budget of a marketing campaign (Khamis et al. 2017).

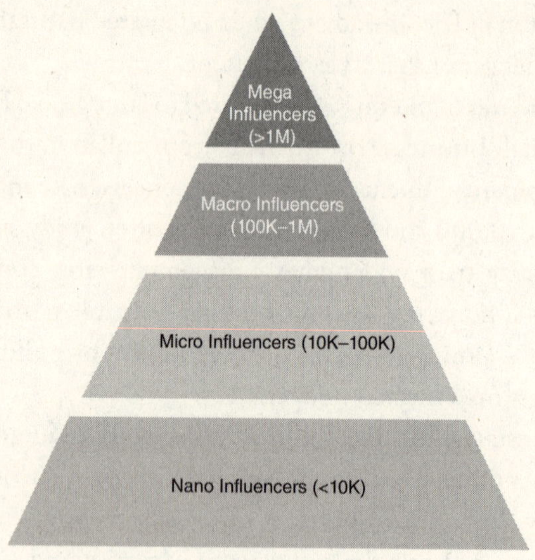

Fig. 7.1: An influencer pyramid chart

- **Mega-influencers:** These are individuals with more than one million followers. They are usually celebrities, actors, athletes, or widely recognized public figures. Mega-influencers can give a brand massive exposure because of their wide reach, but working with them is often expensive. They are best suited for large-scale campaigns that aim to increase brand awareness across broad audiences.
- **Macro-influencers:** Macro-influencers generally have between 100,000 and one million followers. While they may not always be mainstream celebrities, they are highly popular in their niche. Macro-influencers provide significant reach and can help brands build credibility

with diverse audiences, often at a lower cost than mega-influencers.

- **Micro-influencers:** Micro-influencers have between 10,000 and 100,000 followers and typically focus on specific topics, such as fashion, fitness, education, food, or travel. They are known for strong audience connections and high engagement rates since their followers often feel a personal bond with them. Micro-influencers are highly effective for targeting niche markets and delivering more authentic recommendations.
- **Nano-influencers:** Nano-influencers have fewer than 10,000 followers. Although their reach is smaller, their audiences are highly loyal and engaged. Because they are seen as relatable and trustworthy within their close-knit communities, their endorsements often feel more personal and genuine.

Follower vs Engagement Comparison

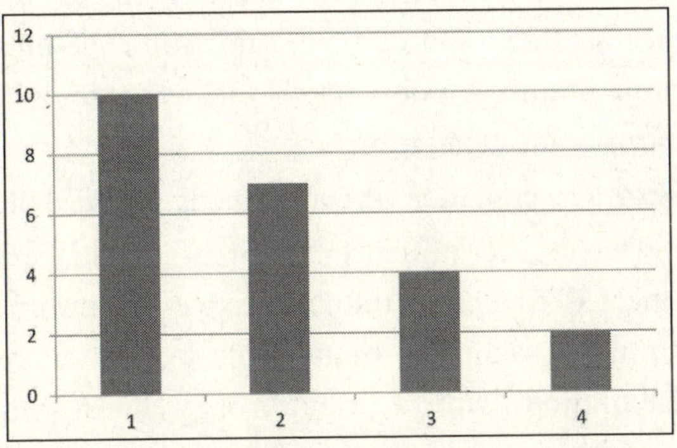

Fig. 7.2: A bar chart comparing engagement rates

Insider Note: For small businesses and start-ups, micro- and nano-influencers are often the most practical choice. They are more affordable to collaborate with, deliver higher engagement, and their recommendations are trusted by their audiences. This makes them especially effective for driving targeted awareness and building meaningful brand connections.

Finding and Vetting the Right Influencers

- ☐ Relevance
- ☐ Engagement
- ☐ Authenticity
- ☐ Audience Fit

Fig. 7.3: Choosing the right influencer

Selecting the right influencer is one of the most crucial steps in building a successful influencer marketing campaign. Having a large follower count alone is not enough. The influencer's values, content style, and audience must align with your brand. A poor match can waste resources and even harm brand reputation.

Key factors to consider when choosing an influencer:

- **Relevance:** The influencer's content should be directly connected to your product, service, or industry. For example, a skincare brand will benefit more from collaborating with a beauty or wellness influencer than with a travel blogger. Relevance ensures that the influencer's audience is already interested in similar topics, increasing the likelihood of positive engagement.

- **Engagement:** Engagement is often more important than the number of followers. Look at how actively the audience interacts with the influencer's content through likes, comments, shares, and replies. High engagement signals that the influencer has built trust and credibility with their audience.
- **Authenticity:** Authenticity is a critical factor in influencer marketing success. Audiences quickly notice when influencers promote too many products without personal experience. Effective influencers share genuine stories, experiences, and opinions that make the promotion feel natural rather than forced (Jin et al. 2019).
- **Audience fit:** The influencer's followers should closely match your target market. For example, if your product is aimed at college students, an influencer with a follower base mainly in the 18–24 age group is a better choice. Analysing demographics such as age, gender, location, and interests ensures that your message reaches the right people.

Insider Note: Instead of only checking follower numbers, always review the influencer's comments section. This helps you understand the real level of interaction and whether the followers are genuine or inactive.

How to Find Influencers

There are two main ways to discover influencers for your campaign:

1. **Manual search:** You can look for influencers directly on social media platforms such as Instagram, YouTube, TikTok, or LinkedIn. Use hashtags, keywords, or location-based searches to identify people creating content in your niche. For example, searching #FitnessTips on Instagram can help you find fitness trainers who regularly post relevant content.
2. **Influencer discovery tools:** To save time and filter options more effectively, you can use influencer discovery platforms such as BuzzSumo, Upfluence, Collabstr, or Heepsy. These tools allow you to search by platform, niche, audience demographics, and engagement rate. Unlike manual search, they provide data-driven insights that make it easier to find influencers who genuinely match your brand goals (Mediakix 2023).

Common Mistakes to Avoid

✖ 1. Choosing by follower count only
✖ 2. Ignoring fake followers
✖ 3. Overlooking relevance
✖ 4. Skipping engagement analysis
✖ 5. Ignoring platform fit
✖ 6. Poor communication

Fig. 7.4 :Top 6 influencer marketing mistakes

Many businesses, especially beginners, make small but costly mistakes when working with influencers. Being aware of these pitfalls can improve campaign success.

1. **Selecting influencers only by follower count:** A high number of followers does not always guarantee results. Micro- and nano-influencers often deliver stronger engagement and deeper trust within their communities compared to mega-influencers.
2. **Ignoring fake followers:** Some influencers boost numbers with fake or inactive accounts. To avoid wasting resources, check engagement quality, comment authenticity, and use tools like Hypeauditor to detect suspicious patterns.
3. **Overlooking relevance:** An influencer must be connected to your industry. For instance, a fashion blogger may not be the right choice to promote an educational course. Relevance ensures the audience is already interested in your product type.
4. **Skipping engagement analysis:** Engagement is one of the strongest indicators of influence. Always review how many likes, comments, and shares the influencer's posts receive. Consistent interaction shows that their audience is active and paying attention.
5. **Ignoring platform fit:** Not all influencers perform equally well across platforms. A LinkedIn professional may excel in B2B campaigns but may not create strong results on Instagram. Always match the influencer's strength with the platform's audience behaviour.

6. **Lack of clear communication:** Many campaigns fail because goals, timelines, or content expectations were not clearly defined. Always share detailed campaign requirements and agree on deliverables beforehand to avoid confusion and poor-quality outcomes.

Campaign Models

Once you have selected the right influencer, the next step is to decide how to work with them. The type of campaign you choose depends on your marketing goals, budget, and the level of involvement you expect from the influencer. Each campaign model has its own benefits. Choose the one that matches your objectives and resources. Even a simple Instagram story or reel from a well-matched influencer can spark interest in your brand and bring in potential customers.

Here are some common influencer marketing models:

- **Sponsored posts:** This is one of the most popular methods. The brand pays the influencer to create and share content about the product or service. These can be Instagram posts, YouTube videos, blog articles, or short reels. Sponsored posts are useful for raising brand awareness or promoting a limited-time offer.
- **Product gifting:** In this model, you send a free product to the influencer and request a review or mention in return. This is often used by small businesses or start-ups with limited budgets. While the post is not guaranteed, many nano- and micro-influencers share honest feedback in exchange for gifts.

- **Takeovers:** The influencer temporarily takes control of your brand's social media account to create and share content. This helps you connect with their followers directly through your page. Takeovers work well for product launches, live events, or Q&A sessions.
- **Collaborations:** Here, the influencer works closely with your brand to co-create a product, campaign, or limited-edition offering. For example, a fashion influencer might help design a clothing line with your brand name. This builds deeper trust with their audience and brings long-term visibility.
- **Affiliate programmes:** The influencer shares a referral link or unique discount code. They earn a commission for every sale made through that link. This model is ideal when your goal is to increase online sales, and you want to pay based on performance.

Types of Content

Influencers use different kinds of content, depending on the platform and the campaign goal. The most effective influencer content feels natural and blends seamlessly with their usual posts so that it does not look like a direct advertisement. Below are the most common formats:

1. **Image or photo posts:** These are high-quality photos featuring the product along with a caption that often shares a personal experience or recommendation. They are especially popular on platforms like Instagram and Facebook, where visuals create strong first impressions.

2. **Short Videos and Reels:** Short-form videos, usually 15 to 90 seconds long, are designed to grab attention quickly. They work well for demonstrating products in action, such as make-up tutorials, fashion try-ons, food recipes, or quick tips. Reels are highly engaging and widely used on Instagram and Facebook.
3. **Stories:** Stories are temporary posts that disappear after 24 hours, unless saved. They are commonly used for real-time updates, behind-the-scenes looks, or product unboxings. Features such as polls, stickers, and links encourage interaction and drive immediate engagement.
4. **YouTube videos:** Longer video formats, such as tutorials, product reviews, vlogs, or 'day in the life' content, allow influencers to explain products in more depth. These videos build stronger trust because followers can see detailed demonstrations and authentic feedback.
5. **Blog posts:** Some influencers also write detailed reviews on personal blogs or partner websites. These posts usually include images, links, and step-by-step explanations. Blog content not only helps with credibility but also improves search engine visibility and generates long-term organic traffic.

Example: When **Mamaearth**® launched its *Vitamin C Face Wash*, the brand collaborated with YouTuber Shreya Jain, a popular beauty influencer. Instead of a short promotional clip, she uploaded a detailed 12-minute review video, explaining the ingredients, texture, scent, and results after two weeks of use. She also demonstrated the product in her skincare routine and compared it with another face wash in the same price range. Viewers appreciated the honest pros and cons, and many commented that they bought the product after watching the review because it felt 'genuine and well-explained'. This example shows how long-form YouTube videos help build deeper trust through authentic storytelling and hands-on demonstrations.

6. **Live Sessions:** Influencers connect with their audience in real time through live streaming on platforms such as Instagram, Facebook, or YouTube. They may unbox products, answer questions, or share personal experiences. Live sessions create authenticity and urgency as followers interact directly during the session.
7. **Giveaways and Contests:** Influencers often host contests where followers participate by liking, sharing, or tagging friends for a chance to win products. This strategy spreads brand awareness quickly, creates excitement, and attracts new potential customers.

Measuring Return on Investment: Engagement, Reach, and Conversions

Measuring the return on investment (ROI) helps you understand whether your influencer campaign achieved the desired results. It also tells you which influencers or content types performed best so you can improve future campaigns. Here are the key performance indicators to track:

- **Reach:** This shows how many unique people saw the influencer's content. A high reach means your brand became visible to a large audience, which is especially useful for brand awareness.
- **Engagement:** This includes the number of likes, comments, shares, saves, or reactions the content received. High engagement means the audience found the post interesting or relatable. It's also a sign of trust and attention.
- **Website Traffic:** If the influencer shared your link or mentioned your website, check how many people visited it during and after the campaign. You can track these using tools like Google Analytics.
- **Sales or Leads:** The most direct way to measure success is to see how many people actually made a purchase, filled out a form, downloaded something, or contacted you after seeing the influencer's post.

To track results more accurately, give each influencer

- a unique discount code (like RICHA20),
- a custom link (like www.yourbrand.com/influencer1).

This helps you identify exactly where leads or sales are coming from. You'll also be able to compare which influencer brought in the most value.

Remember, the success of an influencer campaign is not always about immediate sales. It can also be about building brand visibility, gaining trust, or growing your social media following over time.

Tools for Influencer Discovery

Finding the right influencer manually can be time-consuming, especially for beginners in digital marketing. To simplify this process, several online platforms provide structured ways to discover, evaluate, and connect with influencers. These tools allow searches based on factors such as industry, location, audience size, engagement rate, and type of content, making it easier to identify influencers who align with your brand.

1. **BuzzSumo®:** BuzzSumo is widely used to identify top-performing content and the influencers who create it. By entering keywords or topics, you can see which influencers are driving the highest engagement within your niche. This makes it useful for brands that want to identify thought leaders and analyse trending content.
2. **Upfluence®:** Upfluence is a powerful platform that offers advanced filtering options. Marketers can search for influencers based on industry, social platform, follower count, and engagement rate. It also provides detailed analytics about influencer performance, helping businesses make informed choices before collaboration.
3. **Collabstr®, Heepsy®, and Influencity®:** These tools are more beginner-friendly and are often recommended for start-ups or small businesses. They offer simple dashboards where you can browse influencer profiles, compare pricing, and review sample content. Many of these platforms also provide audience insights to ensure that the influencer's followers match your target market.

Insider Note: If you're just starting out, try the free version or trial of one of these platforms to explore how they work.

Tool	Best For	Key Feature
BuzzSumo	Trending topics	Content analysis
Upfluence	Advanced analytics	Filtering by niche
Heepsy	Small brands	Affordable pricing

Quick Bytes

- Influencer marketing involves partnering with people who already have a loyal social media following to promote your brand in a natural and relatable way.
- Micro- and nano-influencers are often the best choice for small businesses because they are affordable and have strong connections with their audience.
- Always check for relevance, engagement, authenticity, and audience match before choosing an influencer.
- Use promo codes, tracking links, and insights from tools or platforms to measure the success of your campaign.
- Start small, test different approaches, and build long-term relationships with influencers who genuinely support your brand.

Self-Assessment Questions *(For Revision and Reflection)*

1. Why do people tend to trust product recommendations from influencers more than traditional advertisements?

2. If you had a small business, would you work with a micro-influencer or a celebrity influencer? Why?
3. What qualities would you look for before choosing an influencer to represent your brand?
4. Imagine your influencer campaign is not performing well. What possible mistakes might be causing it?
5. How can tools like BuzzSumo or Upfluence help you choose the right influencer and measure campaign success?

References

1. S. V. Jin, A. Muqaddam, and E. Ryu, 'Instafamous and Social Media Influencer Marketing', *Marketing Intelligence & Planning* 37, no. 5 (2019): 567–579.
2. S. Khamis, L. Ang, and R. Welling, '"Self-branding, "Micro-celebrity" and the Rise of Social Media Influencers', *Celebrity Studies* 8, no. 2 (2017): 191–208.
3. Mediakix, 'How to Find Influencers for Your Brand', 2023.
4. Nielsen, *Trust in Advertising Report* (2021).

Chapter 8

Affiliate Marketing Basics

What Is Affiliate Marketing?

Affiliate marketing is a type of performance-based digital marketing where an individual or publisher, known as an affiliate, earns a commission by promoting another company's products or services. The process works through special tracking links that record customer activity. When a user clicks the affiliate link and makes a purchase, the affiliate receives a percentage of the revenue or a fixed payout (Patel 2020). This model has become one of the most popular online income streams because it creates a win-win relationship.

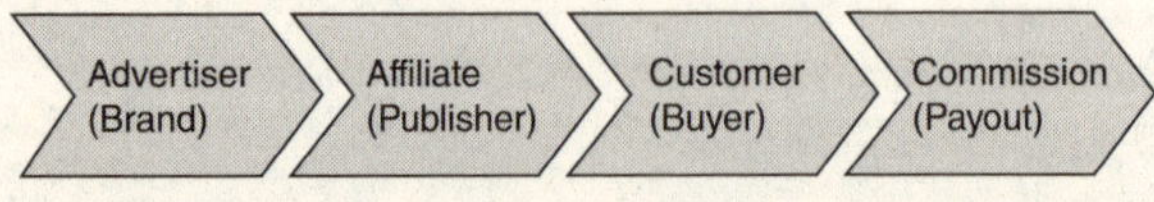

Fig. 8.1: Affiliate marketing model

- **For Businesses,** it is a cost-effective way to acquire new customers since they only pay when a sale, lead, or action is completed. This reduces marketing risk compared to traditional advertising.

- **For Affiliates,** it is a way to monetize their content, platform, or audience without the responsibility of creating, storing, or shipping products.

Affiliate marketing thrives on trust and authenticity. Consumers are more likely to buy when recommendations come from a source they already follow and respect. For this reason, influencers, bloggers, and content creators often integrate affiliate links into their reviews, tutorials, or lifestyle content. It is widely used across platforms such as blogs, YouTube channels, Instagram accounts, and personal websites. Well-established companies like Amazon Associates, Flipkart Affiliate, and MakeMyTrip Affiliate Programme provide unique tracking links for creators. These links can be placed in blog articles, social media posts, video descriptions, or emails.

For beginners, affiliate marketing is particularly attractive because it offers the chance to build passive income. Once the content is published with affiliate links, it can keep generating revenue long after it is created, as long as people continue to engage with the content. Students, bloggers, freelancers, and small businesses can use this strategy to earn extra income while sharing products and services they genuinely recommend. With the global affiliate marketing industry projected to surpass $17 billion (about ₹1,53,000 crore) by 2023 (Statista 2023), it continues to grow as one of the most reliable and scalable online business models for both companies and individuals.

Example scenario: Imagine a travel blogger writes an article about 'Top 10 Budget Hotels in Goa'. In the article, they add affiliate links to hotel booking sites like MakeMyTrip.

- **Advertiser:** MakeMyTrip® pays a commission for bookings made through the affiliate link.
- **Affiliate/Publisher:** The travel blogger earns a commission when a reader clicks the link and books a hotel.

Similarly, a YouTuber reviewing a new laptop can include an Amazon affiliate link in the video description.

- **Advertiser:** Amazon® provides the product and pays commission on sales.
- **Affiliate/Publisher:** YouTube® earns a percentage of the sale when viewers purchase through the link.

How Affiliate Programmes Work

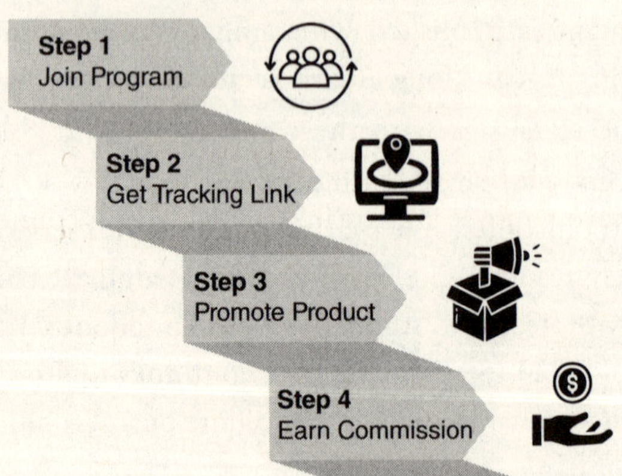

Fig. 8.2: Step-by-step affiliate marketing

Affiliate marketing is one of the simplest models in digital marketing, and anyone can start with very little investment. The process usually follows four key steps.

1. **Join an affiliate programme:** The first step is to register with an affiliate programme run directly by a company or through an affiliate network. Once your application is approved, you become an affiliate partner. Popular options include Amazon Associates®, Flipkart Affiliate®, Commission Junction® (CJ), and ClickBank®. Some companies run their own independent programmes, while others are part of larger networks that host many brands under one platform.

   > An affiliate network acts as a middleman between advertisers (brands or companies) and affiliates (publishers or marketers). It hosts multiple affiliate programmes on one platform, making it easier for affiliates to find products to promote and for advertisers to manage multiple partners.

2. **Get your unique tracking link:** After joining, you receive a unique affiliate link or code that is connected to your account. This link is what tracks customer activity. Whenever someone clicks on your link and takes an action, such as making a purchase or signing up for a service, the system records it. The tracking is done using technologies like cookies and pixels, ensuring the right affiliate gets credit for the sale.

3. **Promote the product or service:** The next step is to share your affiliate link with your audience. This can be done in many ways, depending on the platform you use:
   - A blog post reviewing a product
   - A YouTube video with the link in the description
   - An Instagram story or reel with a 'swipe-up' or 'link in bio'
   - A Facebook or LinkedIn post with recommendations
   - Email newsletters to subscribers
   - WhatsApp or Telegram channels for community-driven promotions

   The key is to integrate the product naturally into your content. Successful affiliates do not just paste links; they create helpful, trustworthy content that encourages people to take action.
4. **Earn a commission:** Finally, when someone clicks on your affiliate link and completes the desired action (such as a purchase, sign-up, or download), you earn a commission. The commission rate depends on the product type and the company. For example,
   - Physical products like books or electronics may offer 2 per cent to 10 per cent commission.
   - Online courses, digital products, or software subscriptions may offer 30 per cent to 50 per cent commission.

- Some companies even pay a recurring commission, meaning you continue to earn as long as the customer keeps renewing their subscription.

This makes affiliate marketing attractive because your income potential can grow over time. Even a single blog post or video can generate commissions for months or years if it keeps attracting viewers.

Example scenario: Imagine you are a student who runs a tech blog. You review a new laptop and add your Amazon affiliate link to the product page. If a reader clicks on your link and buys the laptop, you earn a percentage of the sale. If they buy additional products in the same session (like a mouse or headphones), you earn commissions on those, too.

Affiliate programmes are designed to be simple, trackable, and fair, making them an accessible entry point for beginners who want to earn income online without creating their own products.

Types of Affiliate Content

Affiliates use different types of content to promote products depending on their platform, audience, and personal style. The main goal is to recommend products in a way that feels natural and provides real value. Below are the most common formats.

Fig. 8.3: Affiliates promote products through diverse content formats across multiple platforms

1. **Product Reviews:** Affiliates create written or video reviews that explain the features, benefits, and drawbacks of a product. Honest reviews help build trust and allow the audience to make informed decisions. The affiliate link is usually added for direct purchase.

   Example: A blogger reviews 'The Best Wireless Headphones under ₹5,000' and includes affiliate links to Amazon. Research shows that more than 90 per cent of online shoppers read reviews before purchasing, which makes this format especially powerful.

2. **How-To Guides or Tutorials:** Step-by-step guides demonstrate how to use a product in real life. This type

of content shows the product in action, which builds credibility and encourages adoption.

Example: A YouTuber demonstrates how to use a make-up kit and adds affiliate links to each item used. According to HubSpot (2023), tutorial-style content increases engagement because it solves a specific problem for the audience.

3. **Comparison Posts:** These posts compare two or more products side by side, helping readers decide which option suits them best.

   Example: A blog compares two learning platforms, such as Coursera and Udemy. Since many buyers research multiple options before deciding, comparison content often performs well in search engines (Statista 2023).

4. **Top 10 or List Articles:** List-style content is popular because it is easy to read and covers several options at once.

   Example: 'Top 5 Budget Smartphones for Students – 2025 Edition'. These articles attract high traffic because users often search for 'best' or 'top' lists when exploring purchase options.

5. **Social Media Posts and Stories:** Affiliates also promote products through short and engaging posts on Instagram, Facebook, or WhatsApp. These posts often include quick tips, unboxing videos, or limited-time offers with links such as 'Shop Now'.

Example: An Instagram story shows an unboxing of a gadget with a clickable purchase link. Since social media is one of the top drivers of product discovery, this format is ideal for quick conversions (Hootsuite 2023).

6. **Email Newsletters:** Email marketing allows affiliates to share recommendations directly with subscribers who already trust them. Adding affiliate links in newsletters can be highly effective for promoting tools, books, or seasonal offers.

   Example: Amit, a tech blogger based in Bengaluru, sends a weekly email newsletter to his subscribers about the latest gadgets and software tools. In one edition, he reviews a popular productivity app and includes his affiliate link for premium subscriptions. Many of his readers, who trust his reviews, click the link and purchase the subscription. Through this newsletter, Amit earns around ₹10,000–₹12,000 per month, demonstrating how email marketing can be a profitable channel for affiliates in India.

7. **YouTube Videos or Reels:** Video content lets affiliates showcase a product visually while sharing personal experiences. This format builds trust because viewers can see the influencer using the product in real time.

   Example: A student creates a reel on 'Best Budget Laptops for Online Classes'. Video is especially effective since 82 per cent of global internet traffic comes from video consumption.

Setting Up Your First Affiliate Campaign

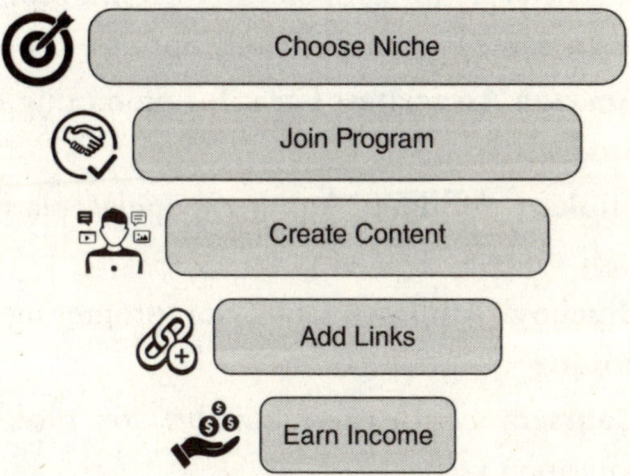

Fig. 8.4: A simple roadmap to launch your first affiliate campaign

Starting your journey in affiliate marketing does not require a lot of technical knowledge or investment. You need the right topic, a platform to share your content, and a little consistency. Follow these beginner-friendly steps to launch your first affiliate campaign.

1. **Choose a Niche:** Pick a topic or industry that you are familiar with or genuinely interested in. It helps if you enjoy talking about the subject as that makes your content more authentic. Common niches include the following:
    - Fitness and wellness
    - Fashion and beauty
    - Books and education
    - Technology and gadgets
    - Personal finance or productivity

2. **Join Affiliate Programmes:** Sign up for affiliate programmes that match your niche. You can choose from general platforms or industry-specific programmes. Here are some beginner-friendly options:
   - **Amazon Associates:** Great for promoting everyday products
   - **Flipkart Affiliate:** Another popular platform for Indian users
   - **Bluehost Affiliate:** Good for promoting website hosting
   - **Coursera or Udemy:** Suitable for those in the education niche

   Most platforms are free to join. Once approved, you'll get access to special tracking links.
3. **Create Useful Content:** Start creating content that adds value to your audience. You can use blogs, YouTube, Instagram, or email newsletters to share your recommendations. Common content formats include the following:
   - Product reviews
   - How-to tutorials
   - Comparison posts
   - 'Top 5' or 'Best of' lists
   - Short Instagram Reels or Stories

   Make sure the content feels helpful rather than overly promotional. Share your personal experience, tips, and honest opinions to build trust.
4. **Insert Affiliate Links:** Add your affiliate link in the right places, either within the text, under videos, or in

your social media bio. The key is to include it where it naturally fits and makes sense for the viewer or reader.

Example: If you're reviewing fitness gear on your blog or YouTube, you can link to specific Amazon products like dumbbells, yoga mats, or protein supplements that you've used or recommend.

Insider Note: Use link shorteners or branded URLs (like bit.ly or yoursite.com/product) to make your links cleaner and easier to share.

Tracking and Payout Models

Affiliate programmes use different models to track performance and pay commissions. Affiliate networks also provide dashboards that allow affiliates to track clicks, conversions, and commissions in real time. This transparency helps affiliates monitor their campaigns and optimize performance. Understanding these models is important because it helps affiliates choose the right programme and set realistic expectations.

Common Affiliate Payment Models

- **Pay Per Sale (PPS):** The most widely used model. Affiliates earn a commission only when someone clicks on their unique link and completes a purchase. Commissions can range from 2 per cent to 50 per cent or more, depending on the product and company (Patel 2023).

- **Pay Per Click (PPC):** Affiliates earn a small payment for every click generated through their links, even if no purchase is made. This model is less common today and typically offers lower payouts.
- **Pay Per Lead (PPL):** Affiliates are paid when a user performs a specific action, such as signing up for a free trial or newsletter or filling out a form. This is especially popular in industries like finance, education, and software.

Table: Comparative infographic table

Model	Example	When Paid	Typical Use
PPS	Amazon product sale	After purchase	E-commerce
PPL	Software sign-up	After sign-up	SaaS
PPC	Click on ad link	Per click	Blogs, ads

Who Decides the Commission?

The commission in an affiliate programme is decided by the advertiser or the company running the affiliate programme. It is usually a fixed percentage of the sale value or a fixed amount per lead or action. In most cases, the commission is not negotiable, especially for large affiliate networks like Amazon or Flipkart, because the rates are standardized across all affiliates. However, for smaller companies or independent programmes, experienced affiliates may sometimes negotiate higher commissions based on their reach, audience quality, or past performance.

How Is the Commission Calculated?

The commission is typically calculated on the final sale price that the customer pays, after discounts, coupons, or offers are applied. It is rarely based on the maximum retail price (MRP). Affiliates should carefully read the programme terms to confirm this as it affects their earnings directly.

Potential Drawbacks and Grey Areas

- If a customer contacts the advertiser directly after seeing a product via an affiliate link, especially for bulk purchases or special rates, the affiliate usually does not earn any commission.
- Some advertisers may offer bulk discounts or special deals that are not tracked through the affiliate link, which can reduce potential earnings for affiliates.
- Affiliates need to be aware that returns, cancellations, or refunds may also affect their commissions as most programmes pay only for completed transactions.

How Payouts Work

- **Minimum Threshold:** Most programmes require affiliates to reach a minimum earning amount, such as ₹500 or $25, before releasing payment.
- **Payout Methods:** Payments are usually made monthly via bank transfer, PayPal, or other online wallets, depending on the programme's policies. Leading platforms like Amazon Associates or Commission

Junction clearly define these rules in their dashboards (Amazon Associates Program Policies 2024).

Real-Time Tracking

Affiliate platforms provide dashboards where you can track key performance data, such as these:

- Number of clicks on your links
- Conversions (sales or sign-ups)
- Commission earned
- Top-performing products or pages

Best Practices for Beginners

Starting with affiliate marketing can be exciting, but success comes from building trust and offering genuine value. Here are some simple tips to keep in mind:

- **Be Honest:** Only promote products or services that you have used, researched, or truly believe in. Your audience will trust your recommendations more if they feel real and personal.
- **Always Disclose Affiliate Links:** Let your readers or viewers know that your content includes affiliate links. A simple note like *This post contains affiliate links, and I may earn a small commission at no extra cost to you* builds transparency and trust.
- **Avoid Over-Promotion:** Do not fill every sentence with a link. Focus on helpful, informative content that educates or solves a problem. A few well-placed links

within valuable content are more effective than constant promotions.

- **Track Performance and Improve:** Use link shorteners like Bitly or add UTM parameters to track which content or platform is getting the most clicks and conversions. This helps you learn what works and what doesn't.

Quick Bytes

- Affiliate marketing allows you to earn income by promoting someone else's product using a unique tracking link.
- You can get started by joining affiliate programmes like Amazon Associates, Flipkart Affiliate, or niche platforms such as Coursera or Bluehost.
- Focus on creating helpful content such as reviews, comparisons, tutorials, or recommendation lists through blogs, YouTube videos, or social media posts.
- Track your performance using affiliate dashboards or link tracking tools and always follow ethical practices by being transparent with your audience.
- With consistent effort, affiliate marketing can grow into a reliable source of passive income over time.

Self-Assessment Questions *(For Revision and Reflection)*

1. Why do you think affiliate marketing has become such a popular way to earn online today?
2. If you were to start your own affiliate campaign, which product or service would you choose, and why?

3. How does trust between an affiliate and their audience affect the success of affiliate marketing?
4. What type of affiliate content, such as reviews, tutorials, or comparisons, do you personally find most convincing?
5. Why is it important to understand tracking and payout models before joining an affiliate programme?

References

1. Amazon, *Amazon Associates Program Policies* (Seattle: Amazon, 2024), Amazon Affiliate Program.
2. Hootsuite and We Are Social, *Digital 2023: Global Overview Report* (Vancouver: Hootsuite, 2023).
3. HubSpot, *The Ultimate List of Marketing Statistics for 2023* (Cambridge, MA: HubSpot, 2023).
4. Neil Patel, *The Beginner's Guide to Affiliate Marketing* (Neil Patel Digital, 2020).
5. Statista, *Affiliate Marketing Spending Worldwide from 2017 to 2023* (Hamburg: Statista, 2023).

Chapter 9

Analytics and Performance Tracking

The Importance of Data in Digital Marketing

Unlike traditional marketing, where results are often difficult to measure, digital marketing provides detailed insights that allow businesses to make informed decisions. For instance, if you run a newspaper or billboard advertisement, it is nearly impossible to know how many people actually paid attention to it. In contrast, digital platforms provide measurable data, such as the number of users who visited your website, clicked on your ad, or purchased a product. According to Chaffey and Smith (2022), data-driven marketing enables brands to not only monitor performance but also to create highly personalized experiences, which significantly improve engagement and customer loyalty.

This ability to measure and analyse is the core strength of digital analytics. By leveraging data, businesses can

- understand their audience's demographics, preferences, and online behaviour,
- identify which content, campaigns, or products perform best, and why,

- save resources by avoiding ineffective strategies and focusing only on what works,
- enhance return on investment (ROI) by optimizing campaigns based on evidence rather than guesswork.

Even simple tracking tools, such as Google Analytics or built-in social media insights, can help small businesses or bloggers measure performance and improve gradually. **For example**, tracking metrics like page views, bounce rate, or traffic sources provides a clearer picture of what attracts and retains visitors. Over time, these insights guide consistent improvement and sustainable growth.

Introduction to Google Analytics 4

Google Analytics 4 (GA4) is a free analytics platform developed by Google that enables businesses, marketers, and website owners to understand how users interact with their websites or mobile applications. By adding a GA4 tracking code (or Google Tag Manager set-up) to your site, data collection begins automatically, giving you access to valuable insights in real time.

GA4 helps answer key questions, such as these:

- How many people visited your website or app within a specific time frame?
- Which pages or screens were viewed most frequently?
- How long did visitors stay and what actions did they take?
- Where did the traffic come from, such as Google Search, Instagram, WhatsApp, or direct visits?

Unlike the older Universal Analytics, GA4 is built on an event-based model rather than session-based tracking. This means every user interaction (for example, clicks, scrolls, video plays, downloads) is recorded as an event, giving marketers more flexibility to track micro-level behaviours. It also provides cross-platform tracking, which allows businesses to see how users move between a website and an app seamlessly.

For beginners, the most useful starting point is the standard reports, which cover:

- **User traffic:** How many visitors are arriving and from which sources
- **Engagement:** How users interact with pages, features, or content
- **Conversions:** Whether visitors completed important goals, such as filling a form, downloading a brochure, or making a purchase

GA4 also integrates with Google Ads, helping you measure how paid campaigns drive traffic and conversions. The platform's predictive analytics features, powered by machine learning, can even forecast which users are more likely to convert in the future (Google 2023). For convenience, Google also provides a GA4 mobile app, allowing business owners to quickly check performance on the go and make faster decisions. The shift to GA4 represents Google's move towards a privacy-first and future-proof measurement system, especially as data regulations tighten and cookies become less reliable. For small businesses and students learning digital marketing, GA4 provides a strong foundation for making data-driven decisions.

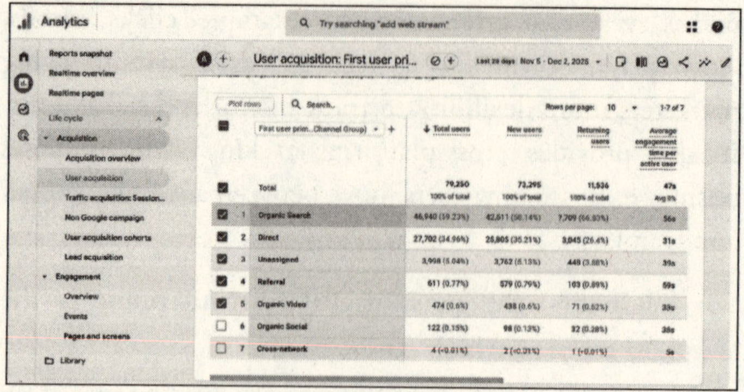

Fig. 9.1: How the GA4 looks like

Key Metrics: CTR, Bounce Rate, and Conversion Rate

Understanding basic performance metrics is one of the most important skills in digital marketing. These indicators show how well your ads or website are performing and help you identify what needs improvement.

- **Click-through rate (CTR):** This measures the percentage of people who clicked your ad or link after seeing it. A higher CTR usually means your ad headline, design, or message is relevant and engaging for your audience.
- **Bounce rate:** This shows the percentage of visitors who left your site without exploring further. A high bounce rate often suggests that the content did not match user expectations, the design was not user-friendly, or the page loaded too slowly.
- **Conversion rate:** This conveys how many visitors completed a desired action, such as filling out a form, subscribing to a newsletter, or purchasing a product.

A higher conversion rate means your website or ad is successfully convincing people to act.

Example: If a thousand people see your ad and 50 click on it, the CTR is 5 per cent. If 10 out of those 50 visitors make a purchase, then the conversion rate is 20 per cent.

SMART Goals and Performance Indicators

Setting **SMART goals** is one of the most effective ways to measure success in digital marketing. SMART stands for:

- **Specific:** Your goal should clearly state what you want to achieve
- **Measurable:** The goal must be tracked with numbers or data
- **Attainable:** It should be realistic and possible with your resources
- **Relevant:** The goal must align with your overall business or marketing objectives
- **Time-bound:** There should be a clear deadline to achieve the goal

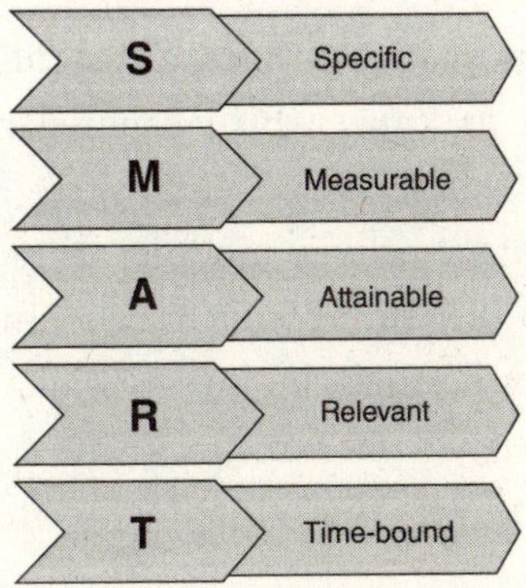

Fig. 9.2: SMART goals

For example,

- Increasing your CTR by 15 per cent within the next two months.
- Reducing the bounce rate on your landing page by 10 per cent in three months.
- Achieving 50 newsletter sign-ups from a single campaign within four weeks.

By setting goals in this structured format, you avoid vague objectives like 'get more sales' and instead work with targets that can be tracked and improved.

Once your goals are set, use analytics dashboards such as Google Analytics 4 (GA4) or Meta Ads Manager to track performance indicators. These tools allow you to see whether your campaigns are meeting the expected benchmarks and also highlight where adjustments are needed. Research shows that marketers who set clear and measurable goals are significantly more likely to achieve better results compared to those who work without defined targets (Chaffey 2022).

UTM Parameters and Campaign Tracking

When you promote your business across different platforms, it is important to know which channel delivers the best results. This is where UTM parameters come in. UTM stands for urchin tracking module. These are short tags that you add to the end of your website links. They do not change the link's destination, but they allow analytics tools such as Google Analytics 4 to track where your visitors are coming from and why they visited your site.

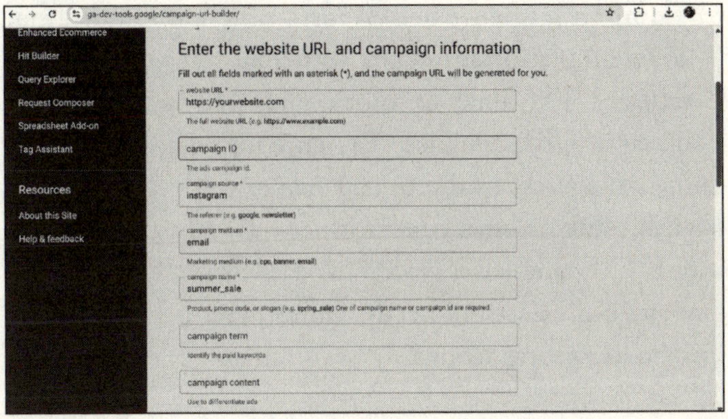

Fig. 9.3: This is how the UTM works

Example:

https://yourwebsite.com?utm_source=instagram&utm_medium=email&utm_campaign=summer_sale

This link tells you that the traffic came from Instagram as part of the summer sale campaign and related to the email campaign.

By using UTM parameters, you can:

- **Identify high-performing platforms:** See whether Instagram®, Facebook®, or Google® Ads bring the most traffic.
- **Measure campaign effectiveness:** Track if a particular ad, email, or influencer post led to more clicks or conversions.
- **Optimize marketing spend:** Instead of guessing, you can invest more money in channels that show better results.

- **Compare audience behaviour:** Learn how visitors from different platforms interact with your website.

Creating UTM links is quick and free with Google's Campaign URL Builder. By entering details such as campaign source, medium, and name, you can generate a trackable link within seconds. Structured campaign tracking with UTM parameters is vital for data-driven marketing as it allows businesses to directly connect user behaviour with specific marketing actions.

Segmenting the Audience

Audience segmentation is the process of dividing a large customer base into smaller groups with shared characteristics. This approach helps businesses deliver more personalized and relevant messages rather than using a one-size-fits-all strategy. Effective segmentation ensures that marketing campaigns reach the right people with the right message at the right time.

Common Segmentation Types

- **Demographics**: Age, gender, education level, income, or occupation. For example, luxury brands may target high-income groups.
- **Location:** Targeting based on city, state, or country. A food delivery app may focus ads only on cities where its service is available.

- **Interests:** Based on hobbies, preferences, or online searches. For instance, a fitness brand may target people who follow workout pages.
- **Behaviour:** Analysing customer actions such as website visits, time spent on a page, abandoned carts, or past purchases. This helps businesses re-target customers with tailored offers.

By understanding these audience segments, businesses can design campaigns that feel more personal, increase engagement, and improve conversions. According to Kotler and Keller (2016), segmentation is a key step in identifying and serving customer needs effectively, making it central to modern marketing strategies.

Understanding Conversion Metrics

A conversion is any action a visitor takes that meets your marketing goal, such as submitting a form, signing up for a course, or completing a purchase.

Conversion Rate = (Number of Conversions/Total Visitors) × 100

If your site had a hundred visitors and ten people made a purchase, your conversion rate would be 10 per cent.

Improving conversion rates is key to success. You can use:

- A/B testing to see which version of a webpage performs better
- Heatmaps and user session recordings to understand visitor behaviour

- Clear calls-to-action and user-friendly layouts to boost performance

Reporting for Beginners

You do not need advanced or complicated reports to start analysing your digital marketing performance. The key is to focus on a few basic metrics and review them regularly. Even simple reporting can provide valuable insights into what is working and what needs improvement.

Key Metrics to Track

- **Visitor count or impressions:** Shows how many people saw your ad, post, or website. This helps you measure overall reach.
- **Clicks and click-through rate:** Indicates how many people interacted with your ad or link after seeing it. A higher CTR means your content is attracting attention.
- **Conversions:** Measures how many people completed a specific goal, such as filling out a form, downloading a brochure, or making a purchase.
- **Cost per result:** Tells you how much you are spending for each desired action, making it easier to check if your campaign is cost-effective.

Best Practice for Beginners

Check these numbers on a weekly or biweekly basis rather than daily. Frequent small reviews help you spot trends without feeling overwhelmed by constant fluctuations. Over time, this habit allows you to make data-driven decisions, optimize your campaigns, and steadily improve results. As Google Analytics documentation notes, starting with simple reports and gradually moving to advanced analysis is the best way for beginners to grow their understanding of digital performance (Google Analytics Help 2023).

Mini Section: Introduction to CRM Tools

What Is a Customer Relationship Management?

A customer relationship management (CRM) tool is software that helps businesses manage all interactions and relationships with customers in one central place. Instead of relying on scattered notes, spreadsheets, or multiple apps, a CRM stores important customer details such as phone numbers, email conversations, purchase history, and reminders for follow-ups in an organized manner. Modern CRMs are more than digital address books. They serve as complete platforms for managing the entire customer journey, from the first interaction to long term relationship building.

How CRMs Support Marketing

A CRM system plays a key role in marketing because it helps businesses understand, segment, and engage with their audience more effectively. Some important benefits are:

- **Tracking customer interactions:** Every call, email, or message with a customer is recorded. This ensures no communication is missed and helps in building trust.

- **Audience segmentation:** Customers can be grouped based on interests, location, or buying behaviour. For example, separating new buyers from loyal customers allows you to send more personalized messages.
- **Automation of campaigns:** CRMs allow automated follow ups, promotional messages, or reminders to be sent at the right time without manual effort.
- **Lead to conversion monitoring:** From the moment a person shows interest until they make a purchase, CRMs track each stage. This makes it easier to identify gaps and improve strategies.

Example: Suppose a campaign generates a hundred leads. With a CRM, you can divide them into groups such as 40 who opened your emails, 30 who clicked on your offers, and 10 who made a purchase. This way, you can send targeted follow-ups to each group, which increases the chance of conversion. Tools such as HubSpot CRM and Zoho CRM are popular with beginners and small businesses. They provide free plans and easy-to-use dashboards, making customer management simple and effective.

Beginner-Friendly Tools

You do not need expensive tools to get started with CRM. Many platforms offer free plans that are ideal for small businesses and beginners.

- **HubSpot® CRM:** Offers a simple dashboard and features like email tracking, contact management, and task reminders. It is free and easy to use.

- **Zoho® CRM:** Good for growing teams, this platform includes lead tracking, email automation, and integration with popular tools.

Both platforms are cloud-based and work well with tools like Gmail, Google Ads, and Facebook.

CRM Tool vs Spreadsheets

Let us compare CRM tools with traditional spreadsheets:

Feature	Spreadsheet	CRM Tool
Manual entry	✓ Required	✖ Mostly automated
Follow-up reminders	✖ Not available	✓ Built-in
Customer history	✖ Hard to manage	✓ Auto-recorded
Campaign tracking	✖ Limited	✓ Integrated
Team collaboration	✖ Difficult	✓ Easy sharing

As your business grows, spreadsheets become harder to manage. CRM tools help you to stay organized, save time, and improve your marketing results.

Quick Bytes

- Analytics provide insights to measure performance and improve campaigns.
- Google Analytics 4 (GA4) is a free tool that tracks website and app activity.
- Key metrics like CTR, bounce rate, and conversion rate reveal user behaviour and campaign effectiveness.
- UTM parameters help identify which channels or campaigns drive the most traffic.

- Audience segmentation allows more relevant communication, leading to stronger engagement and better results.
- CRM tools like HubSpot® and Zoho® organize customer data more effectively than spreadsheets and support smarter marketing decisions.

Self-Assessment Questions *(For Revision and Reflection)*

1. What is the main advantage of digital marketing analytics compared to traditional marketing?
2. What does GA4 help businesses understand about their website or app users?
3. What do the terms CTR, bounce rate, and conversion rate measure in digital marketing?
4. What does the SMART framework stand for in goal setting?
5. Why do businesses use CRM tools instead of spreadsheets for managing customer information?

References

1. Dave Chaffey and P. R. Smith, *Digital Marketing Excellence: Planning, Optimizing and Integrating Online Marketing*, 7th ed. (London: Routledge, 2022).
2. Google, *Analytics Help: Get Started with Google Analytics 4* (Google, 2023).
3. Philip Kotler and Kevin Lane Keller, *Marketing Management*, 15th ed. (Harlow: Pearson Education, 2016).

Chapter 10

Creating a Digital Marketing Strategy

Strategy vs Campaign?

One of the most common mistakes beginners make in digital marketing is confusing a strategy with a campaign. While the two are closely related, they serve different purposes and operate at different levels of planning. A digital marketing strategy is the big-picture and long-term plan. It defines what you want to achieve online, who your target audience is, what key message you want to communicate, and which platforms or tools you will use to reach your goals. It acts as a road map, guiding all your marketing decisions and ensuring consistency across efforts. A good strategy is rooted in business objectives, whether it is to increase brand awareness, generate leads, or drive online sales (Chaffey and Smith 2017).

A digital marketing campaign, on the other hand, is a short-term, focused activity designed to support the overall strategy. Campaigns usually have a specific purpose, such as promoting a product launch, running a seasonal sale, or generating sign-ups for an event. They are tactical in nature, often time-bound, and measurable in their results.

Example: Suppose you run a bakery. Your strategy might be to increase brand awareness in your city over the next six months by using Instagram and Google Ads. To achieve this, you may run several campaigns, such as a three-day Instagram promotion offering discounts on birthday cakes or a Google Ads campaign targeting 'best cupcakes near me.' These campaigns are the building blocks that support your long-term strategy.

Aspect	**Digital Marketing Strategy**	**Digital Marketing Campaign**
Definition	Long-term plan that guides all digital marketing efforts	Short-term, focused action that supports the strategy
Duration	Ongoing (months or years)	Limited time frame (days, weeks, months)
Focus	Big-picture goals (e.g., brand awareness, lead generation)	Specific objectives (e.g., promote a new product, increase sign-ups)
Scope	Broad, covering multiple channels and tactics	Narrow, targeting one specific activity or audience
Measurement	Success measured by overall growth and alignment with business objectives	Success measured by campaign-specific key performance indicators – KPIs (e.g., clicks, conversions, sales)
Example	Build online visibility through SEO and social media over six months	Run a Diwali discount campaign for three days on Instagram

Setting SMART Goals

Before you choose platforms, create content, or allocate a budget, it is essential to be clear about what you are trying to achieve. Vague objectives like '*get more sales*' or '*grow my Instagram*' may sound appealing, but they are not measurable or trackable. This is where the SMART goal framework becomes highly useful. SMART is an acronym that helps you set goals that are structured and actionable (Doran 1981; Chaffey and Ellis-Chadwick 2019). This has been discussed in the previous chapter.

Selecting the Right Channels

Not every digital channel is equally effective for all businesses. Choosing the right platforms depends on your audience behaviour, product type, content format, and resources. Selecting wisely ensures that your efforts generate meaningful results instead of being spread too thin.

1. Where your audience is active

- **Gen Z:** Platforms like Instagram, YouTube, and Snapchat are highly popular among younger audiences.
- **Working professionals:** LinkedIn is the go-to platform for B2B networking and professional services.
- **Families or older users:** Facebook and WhatsApp are widely used by older age groups for daily communication and community engagement.

2. Type of product or service

- **Local services (such as salons, gyms, tutors):** Perform better with Google Ads, Google Maps, or WhatsApp marketing, where users often search locally.
- **Visual products (such as fashion, beauty, or food):** Do well on Instagram, Pinterest, and YouTube, where visual storytelling is central.

3. Content format

- **Short videos:** Instagram Reels, TikTok, and YouTube Shorts are ideal for quick, engaging content.
- **Long-form written content:** Blogs and SEO-driven articles help attract organic traffic through Google Search.

4. Your time and budget

Small businesses or start-ups should begin with one or two key channels to avoid overextension. Monitor performance and gradually expand once you see consistent results.

Example: A fitness trainer may choose Instagram (for Reels and workout tips) and YouTube (for long tutorials). Over time, they may expand to a blog for SEO or LinkedIn to connect with professionals.

Common Beginner Combinations

Goals	Suggested Channels
Build brand awareness	Instagram, YouTube, Google Display Ads
Generate leads	Google Search Ads, Facebook Lead Ads
Drive website traffic	SEO, Google Ads, Facebook Ads
Build community/engagement	Instagram, Facebook, WhatsApp, LinkedIn

> **Insider Note:** Start where your audience already spends time. Build one channel well before trying to manage many.

Sample Strategy for a Local Business

Creating a digital marketing strategy for a local business does not need to be complicated. The key is to start small, focus on the right audience, and use cost-effective tools.

Here's is an example:

Business Type: Yoga studio in Jaipur

Goal: Generate 50 new leads in one month

Target Audience: Women aged 25–45 living in Jaipur

Digital Channels:

- **Google Search Ads:** To capture intent-based searches such as 'Yoga classes in Jaipur'
- **Instagram:** To build awareness through engaging visual content

Actions:

1. **Google Ads Campaign**
   - Use targeted keywords like *yoga classes near me*, *yoga for beginners Jaipur*, and *best yoga studio in Jaipur*.
   - Direct traffic to a simple landing page or Google Form to collect leads.
2. **Instagram Marketing**
   - Share short Reels on yoga tips, wellness routines, and testimonials from existing students.

- Post highlights of live classes to build credibility and attract followers.
- Use hashtags such as *#YogaInJaipur* and *#Jaipur Wellness* to increase reach.

3. **Lead Capture**
   - Use a Google Form or a simple landing page with a clear call to action (CTA), such as *'Book a Free Trial Class'*.
   - Collect name, phone number, and email to follow up via WhatsApp or email campaigns.

Budget: ₹5,000 allocated for ads (₹3,500 for Google Ads and ₹1,500 for Instagram boosts).

Tools: Google Ads, Instagram, Google Forms, Canva (for designing posters and posts).

Why this works:

- It focuses on a local audience instead of wasting money on irrelevant clicks.
- It uses affordable, beginner-friendly tools.
- It sets a specific and measurable goal (50 leads in 30 days).

Budgeting Basics

You do not need a large budget to begin digital marketing. What matters most is how wisely you use your money and time. A well-planned budget ensures that even small investments can generate meaningful results.

Key Budgeting Principles for Beginners

- **Start small:** Begin with a modest ad spend of ₹100–₹200 per day. This allows you to test which ads, platforms, or content types perform best before scaling up.
- **Use Free Tools:** Platforms like Canva (design), CapCut (video editing), Google Forms (lead collection), and Instagram (organic promotion) help you create professional content without upfront costs.
- **Budget your time:** Allocate a few hours each week for creating content, engaging with followers, and reviewing analytics. Consistency matters more than spending heavily.
- **Focus on return on investment (ROI):** Do not spend money simply to gain likes or followers. Invest in activities that generate leads, sign-ups, or actual purchases.
- **Track every expense:** Use a simple spreadsheet or a free tool like Google Sheets to record daily spending and results. Tracking ensures you know what works and prevents overspending.

Monitoring and Adjusting Your Strategy

A strong digital marketing strategy is not static. It evolves based on performance, customer behaviour, and changes in the market. Continuous monitoring ensures that your efforts remain effective and that your budget is being spent wisely. Flexibility and data-driven decision-making allow you to scale what works and improve what does not.

How to Monitor and Adjust Effectively

- **Track performance:** Use tools such as GA4 to measure website traffic and conversions, Meta Ads Manager for campaign insights, or Instagram Insights for post reach and engagement.
- **Review consistently:** Check results weekly or biweekly to identify trends. Focus on your best-performing posts, campaigns, or ads and understand why they worked.
- **Tweak your approach:** Adjust targeting, budget, ad creatives, or posting times based on performance. Even small changes can significantly improve results over time.
- **Experiment with A/B testing:** Run simple tests, such as comparing two different headlines, call-to-action buttons, or images, to find which performs better.
- **Listen to your audience:** Comments, direct messages, and shares provide real-time feedback on what resonates with your audience. Incorporating these inputs strengthen your connection with them.

Quick Bytes

- A strategy is your long-term digital marketing road map, while a campaign is a short-term, focused effort within that plan.
- Use the SMART framework to set goals that are clear, measurable, and time-bound.
- Select digital channels based on your audience, content type, and business objectives.
- Start with a simple, low-budget plan (like the yoga studio example) to test and learn.

- Invest your time and money in platforms that deliver the highest returns.
- Review and adjust regularly to keep your strategy effective and aligned with your goals.

Self-Assessment Questions *(For Revision and Reflection)*

1. What is the difference between a digital marketing strategy and a marketing campaign?
2. What does the SMART framework help businesses do?
3. Why is selecting the right digital platforms important for a marketing strategy?
4. What is the purpose of setting a daily or monthly marketing budget?
5. Why is monitoring and optimizing important after launching a marketing plan?

References

1. Dave Chaffey and P. R. Smith, *Digital Marketing Excellence: Planning, Optimizing and Integrating Online Marketing* (London: Routledge, 2017).
2. George T. Doran, 'There's a S.M.A.R.T. Way to Write Management's Goals and Objectives', *Management Review* 70, no. 11 (1981): 35–36.
3. Dave Chaffey and Fiona Ellis-Chadwick, *Digital Marketing*, 7th ed. (Harlow: Pearson Education, 2019).

Chapter 11

AI for Content Creation

What Is AI in Digital Marketing?

Artificial Intelligence (AI) in digital marketing refers to the use of smart technologies that can analyse data, generate ideas, and create content automatically. It helps marketers and businesses understand customer behaviour, personalize communication, and produce marketing materials more efficiently.

AI tools can write text, design images, create videos, and even suggest strategies based on user input. In simple terms, AI acts like a virtual assistant that saves time and helps marketers focus on creative and strategic work. According to McKinsey (2023), AI is transforming digital marketing by improving accuracy, increasing productivity, and helping companies deliver better customer experiences.

Example: A small business owner can use AI tools to write product descriptions, design social media posts, or edit videos without needing professional help. This has made digital marketing more accessible, even for beginners and non-technical users.

Benefits of Using AI for Beginners

AI offers several benefits to beginners in digital marketing. It simplifies complex tasks, reduces time, and enhances creativity. The main advantages include:

1. **Speed:** AI tools can create a blog post, design, or video script within minutes. What once took hours can now be done in a fraction of the time.
2. **Idea generation:** Beginners often struggle with where to start. AI tools like ChatGPT or Copy.ai can suggest content ideas, catchy captions, ad headlines, or blog outlines instantly.
3. **Visual creation:** Design tools like Canva AI and Pictory help create attractive graphics or short videos even without advanced design skills.
4. **Scaling up:** AI makes it possible to produce more content in less time. This helps businesses grow faster and maintain a consistent online presence.

The Human Touch Is Necessary

Artificial Intelligence is a helpful tool, but it cannot replace human creativity and thinking. AI can quickly generate text, images, and videos, but when used without changes, the content often looks robotic, repetitive, or shallow. Today, many people can easily recognize AI-generated content and may ignore it if it feels unnatural or generic.

AI should mainly be used for ideas, outlines, and inspiration. Students and marketers should always review, edit, and personalize AI output before using it. Copying

AI content directly can reduce engagement and damage credibility.

There is also a risk of plagiarism. AI tools learn from existing content, so the output may closely match already published material. Using such content without changes can create ethical and legal problems.

The best approach is to use AI as a support system. Write your own content, create original designs, and use real photographs or videos wherever possible. Adding personal examples, real experiences, and emotional elements makes content more authentic and trustworthy.

In short, AI can assist your work, but meaningful content still needs human ideas, originality, and responsibility.

Common AI Tools for Content Creation

Artificial intelligence tools have transformed how marketers, students, and entrepreneurs create content. They help in writing, designing, editing, and even producing videos, making digital marketing faster and easier for everyone, especially beginners. According to HubSpot's Global Marketing Report (2024), more than 60 per cent of marketers now use AI tools to streamline writing, design tasks, and content planning. Let us look at some widely used AI tools that can support different aspects of content creation.

ChatGPT **Canva AI** **Grammarly** **Pictory** **Copy.ai**

Fig. 11.1: Popular AI Tools: Write, Design, Edit, Video, Ads

AI tools have become essential for marketers today. Here are some popular and beginner-friendly options:

1. ChatGPT®: Writing and Ideation Assistant

ChatGPT, developed by OpenAI, is one of the most popular AI tools used in digital marketing. It helps users generate ideas, write blog posts, create social media captions, draft emails, or develop marketing copy in just a few seconds.

By giving the tool a clear prompt, such as 'Write a 150-word blog introduction about the importance of SEO for small businesses', users can instantly receive relevant and well-structured content.

Key uses:

- Blog writing and article drafting
- Generating topic ideas and outlines
- Writing social media captions or ad copy
- Creating email campaigns and newsletters
- Simplifying technical content for wider audiences

Tip: Always review AI-generated text to ensure accuracy, and add your personal or brand-specific tone before publishing.

2. Canva AI®: Design and Visual Creation

Canva has integrated several AI features that make graphic design easy for beginners. Its *Magic Write* tool helps users generate captions or text for designs, while *Text to Image* converts written prompts into visuals or illustrations. Users can design posters, flyers, infographics, and social media posts within minutes, even without prior design experience.

Key features:

- *Magic Write* for automatic text generation
- *Text to Image* for creating visuals from descriptions
- *Brand Kit* for maintaining consistent colours, logos, and fonts
- Ready-made templates for social media, presentations, and ads

Example: Type 'Create a poster for a coffee shop offering a weekend discount' into Canva's AI prompt box, and it will generate professional templates complete with graphics and text suggestions.

3. Grammarly® and QuillBot®: Editing and Refinement Tools

Good content must not only look appealing but also read well. Tools like Grammarly and QuillBot are designed to improve writing quality by checking grammar, punctuation, sentence structure, and readability.

- **Grammarly** highlights grammatical and stylistic errors, suggests vocabulary improvements, and adjusts tone depending on the target audience. It is ideal for checking emails, blog posts, and reports.

- **QuillBot** helps with paraphrasing and rewriting sentences to make them clearer or more formal. It is often used by students and writers to avoid repetition and improve clarity.

Tip: These tools are great for editing, but final proofreading by a human ensures the message sounds natural and aligned with your brand's voice.

4. Pictory®: Video Creation and Editing Tools

Video content has become one of the most engaging forms of digital marketing. Tools like Lumen5 and Pictory make video creation easy by converting text into videos automatically. For example, if you paste a blog or article into these tools, they can summarize it and create short video clips using stock images, text animations, and background music.

Key features:

- Turn articles, blogs, or scripts into videos automatically
- Choose from multiple themes, voice-overs, and soundtracks
- Edit text, scenes, and visuals without advanced technical skills
- Ideal for creating promotional videos, explainers, and social media reels

Example: A small boutique can use Pictory to turn its blog post about 'Summer Fashion Trends' into a short Instagram video highlighting new arrivals.

5. Copy.ai® and Jasper®: Advertising and Copywriting Tools

Creating catchy and persuasive advertising copy is often challenging. Tools like Copy.ai and Jasper specialize in writing marketing content that attracts and converts customers. They are widely used by agencies, freelancers, and small business owners for creating ad copy, slogans, and product descriptions.

Key uses:

- Writing Facebook or Google ad copy
- Generating product descriptions for e-commerce sites
- Crafting marketing slogans or taglines
- Creating social media captions tailored to the audience

Example: You can prompt Jasper with 'Write a 30-word Facebook ad promoting handmade jewellery for festive occasions', and it will generate multiple creative options to choose from.

6. Other Useful AI Tools for Marketers

Apart from the popular ones, several other AI tools are gaining popularity among digital marketers:

- **Surfer SEO:** Optimizes blog content for better search rankings.
- **Writesonic:** Creates blogs, landing pages, and ad copy with SEO-friendly keywords.
- **Descript:** Edits videos and podcasts by modifying the text transcript directly.
- **Notion AI:** Helps in brainstorming ideas, writing notes, and planning content calendars.

These tools allow marketers to work smarter, save time, and maintain professional quality across different platforms.

How to Use AI Tools Effectively

AI tools are most powerful when used with clear instructions, known as prompts. A prompt tells the AI exactly what you need. The better the prompt, the better the result.

Tips:

- Be specific. Instead of saying, 'Write a blog on digital marketing,' say, 'Write a 200-word introduction on why digital marketing is important for small businesses.'
- Give context. Mention your target audience, tone, and purpose.
- Review and refine. Always check AI-generated content for accuracy, grammar, and tone.
- Combine tools. You can write using ChatGPT, design with Canva, and check grammar with Grammarly.

Example Prompt: 'Write a short LinkedIn post explaining how AI tools like ChatGPT and Canva help beginners create professional content.'

Limitations and Ethical Considerations

While AI is a powerful assistant, it has limitations and should be used responsibly.

- **Accuracy issues:** AI may sometimes produce incorrect or outdated information, so users should always verify facts.
- **Lack of human emotion:** AI cannot fully replicate human creativity, empathy, or cultural understanding.

- **Data privacy:** Some AI tools store user data. It is important to read privacy policies and avoid sharing sensitive information.
- **Plagiarism risks:** AI-generated text might resemble existing content. Always edit and make it original before publishing.

Ethically, marketers should use AI to assist, not replace, human creativity and honesty. Businesses must disclose if AI is used in customer interactions or content creation to maintain transparency and trust.

Tips for Blending Human Creativity with AI

AI can generate ideas and save time, but true success in digital marketing depends on the human touch. To achieve the best results:

1. Use AI for research and structure, but add your own creativity, stories, and personal examples.
2. Edit and proofread AI-generated content to ensure clarity and accuracy.
3. Maintain your unique brand voice and values in every message.
4. Experiment with prompts and creative inputs to get more personalized outcomes.
5. Keep learning about new AI tools and features to stay updated.

When AI efficiency is combined with human creativity and judgment, the result is impactful, high-quality digital content that connects with the audience.

Quick Bytes

- AI analyses data, generates ideas, and creates content automatically.
- It makes marketing faster and more efficient.
- Beginners gain speed, ideas, visuals, and can scale content.
- Popular tools include ChatGPT, Canva AI, Grammarly, QuillBot, Pictory, Copy.ai, and Jasper.
- Use clear prompts, provide context, review output, and combine tools.
- AI can be inaccurate, lacks human emotion, may risk data privacy, and can plagiarize.
- Always assist AI with human creativity, personal stories, and brand voice.

Self-Assessment Questions *(For Revision and Reflection)*

1. Define AI in digital marketing and explain how it helps beginners in content creation.
2. List three AI tools used for visual or video content creation and explain one key feature of each.
3. What is a prompt in AI content creation, and why is it important for generating better results?
4. Explain two ethical considerations that digital marketers must keep in mind when using AI.
5. How can beginners combine human creativity with AI to produce high-quality content? Give two examples.

Reference

1. HubSpot Research, *State of Marketing Report* (Cambridge, MA: HubSpot, 2024).
2. McKinsey & Company, *The State of AI in 2023* (New York: McKinsey Global Institute, 2023).

Chapter 12

Case Studies and Practical Applications

Digital marketing is best understood not just through theory but by seeing how individuals and businesses apply it in real situations. Case studies bridge the gap between learning and doing, showing what works, what doesn't, and how small decisions can make a big difference. In this chapter, we examine reallife examples of how companies used digital marketing strategies to grow their brand presence, attract customers, and achieve measurable results.

Case Study 1 – Mamaearth: Building a DigitalFirst Direct-to-Consumer Brand with Influencer and Social Media Strategy

Background

Mamaearth was founded in 2016 as a direct-to-consumer (DTC) brand offering baby care products, later expanding into skincare, haircare, and wellness categories. The founders chose an onlinefirst strategy instead of relying heavily on traditional retail. They invested early in digital presence:

website, social media, ecommerce platforms, and content marketing. Source: *The Economic Times+1.*

Strategy: Social Media + Influencer Marketing + Storytelling

1. **Social media engagement:** Mamaearth used platforms like Instagram, Facebook, and YouTube to share relatable, lifestyle-oriented content rather than just product adverts. Posts included parenting tips, daily routines, user testimonials, ingredient education, and behind-the-scenes glimpses. This content helped build a community, not just a customer base. Source: *blog.kirnanitechnologies.com+2Hobo.Video+2.*
2. **Influencer collaborations and user-generated content (UGC):** Rather than only high-end celebrity endorsements, Mamaearth leveraged microinfluencers, parenting bloggers, skincare enthusiasts, and real customers. Through campaigns like '#GoodnessInside' and '#GlowWithMamaearth', they encouraged users to share honest reviews, unboxing videos, before-and-after stories, and daily usage, generating authentic content that resonated more than polished ads. Source: *Hobo.Video+2irt.shodhsagar.com+2.*
3. **Dynamic and datadriven ads:** When using paid advertising (via social ads), Mamaearth employed dynamic product ads and 'discovery commerce' solutions. This helped re-target users based on their browsing history or past interest, delivering personalized

ads to people likely to convert. They adopted a 'test-and-learn' approach: A/B testing creatives, CTAs, and campaign formats, continuously optimizing for conversions. Source: *The Economic Times+1.*

Outcomes and Impact

- The brand achieved rapid growth: from a niche babycare label in 2016 to becoming a large national DTC brand with hundreds of products and a wide consumer reach. Source: *blog.kirnanitechnologies.com+1.*
- Their heavy reliance on digital-first marketing helped them reach millions of customers, even during periods when offline retail was disrupted (for example, during pandemic-related lockdowns). Source: *The Strategy Story+1.*
- The use of authentic influencer content and customer stories built trust among target audiences (especially young parents and millennials), helping convert social media followers into loyal customers. Source: *irt.shodhsagar.com+2Hobo.Video+2.*

Key Lessons for Marketers and Small Businesses

- **Community over ads:** Building a brand identity and community, not just pushing products, can create long-term loyalty.
- **Leverage micro-influencers and real users:** Authentic reviews and user-generated content often perform better than overly polished ads.

- **Combine organic with data-driven ads:** Use social media for brand-building and storytelling; complement with targeted ads to capture intent and convert interest.
- **Rapid scaling even with limited resources:** A digital-first approach reduces dependence on physical retail infrastructure; ideal for start-ups and small businesses.

Case Study 2 – Lenskart: Using Search-Based Advertising to Capture High-Intent Traffic

Background

Lenskart is a major eyewear retailer in India, offering glasses, sunglasses, and contact lenses. While they do have physical stores, a significant portion of their growth has come via online sales and digital marketing. Source: *about.ads.microsoft.com*

Strategy: Pay-per-Click/Search Ads to Target People Searching for Eyewear

- Lenskart leveraged search-based advertising to capture users who are already searching actively. By using keywords like 'buy eyeglasses online', 'best sunglasses India', and 'spectacle lenses near me', they ensured their ads appeared when demand was explicit. Source: *about.ads.microsoft.com*
- Their ad campaigns were optimized for return on ad spend (ROAS). Through targeted ads across search engines, combined with clear landing pages, product catalogues, and easy purchase flows, they aimed for

efficient conversions, reducing cost per acquisition while scaling sales. Source: *about.ads.microsoft.com*

Outcomes and Impact

- According to their advertising partner data, Lenskart's campaign resulted in a 'significant increase in ROAS', meaning their ads yielded good returns relative to spending. Source: about.ads.microsoft.com
- By focusing on search-intent ads rather than broad social campaigns, Lenskart tapped directly into users with purchase intent, thus improving conversion rates and lowering wasted ad spend.
- The strategy helped reinforce brand visibility in the eyewear segment, especially for users looking for affordable yet quality eyewear online.

Key Lessons

- **Search ads = high intent users:** For product categories or services where the customer already knows what they want (like eyewear, electronics, services), search-based advertising often delivers better conversion than broad social campaigns.
- **Optimize for ROI, not just reach:** Focusing on ROAS rather than vanity metrics (likes, shares) ensures marketing spends translate to revenue.
- **Complement digital with offline presence (if available):** Brands with both offline and online footprints can use search ads to drive online orders, especially from customers who prefer convenience.

Case Study 3 – Lendingkart: How Google Ads Helped Grow Qualified Leads for a Fintech Lending Platform

Background

Lendingkart is a fintech company providing business loans and financial services to small and medium enterprises (SMEs) in India. As a service-based business, their challenge was to reach business owners actively seeking loans, a relatively niche but high-intent audience. Source: upGrowth.

Strategy: Targeted Google Ads Campaigns to Generate Leads

- They worked with a growth marketing agency that restructured their Google Ads campaigns, optimizing ad spend, keywords, and targeting for qualified leads rather than general traffic. Source: upGrowth.
- The focus was on improving lead quality and reducing cost per lead (CPL). By refining their ad strategy, selecting more precise keywords, improving ad copy, and optimizing landing pages, they aimed to get more conversions (loan inquiries/applications) per ad spend unit. Source: upGrowth.

Outcomes and Impact

- The campaign produced a **20 per cent business growth** for Lendingkart, attributed to improved ad performance. Source: upGrowth
- Cost per qualified lead dropped by approximately 32.6 per cent, indicating a more efficient acquisition funnel. Source: upGrowth.

- Total conversions increased by 54 per cent compared to previous results, showing that better targeting and campaign management significantly improved ROI. Source: upGrowth.

Key Lessons

- **Service-based businesses benefit from targeted ads:** For offers like loans, coaching, or professional services, where users actively search Google Ads (or search-based campaigns), targeted ads can deliver high-quality leads.
- **Don't just aim for impressions – optimize conversions:** Refining keywords, ad copy, landing pages, and user flow are critical for maximizing ROI.
- **Small budgets can still deliver results:** With disciplined spending and optimization, even moderate ad budgets can result in meaningful growth.

What These Cases Show: Common Patterns and Practical Takeaways

From the three real-world examples above, several common threads and actionable insights emerge.

- **Match approach to audience intent:** If your audience is actively searching (for example, for loans, eyewear, services), search ads often work better. For lifestyle, trust-building, or awareness-driven products (for example, beauty, personal care), social media + influencer marketing + content works well.
- **Leverage authenticity and community-building:** As seen in Mamaearth's example, real user stories, honest

testimonials, and micro-influencers build trust faster than polished advertising.

- **Optimize spend for ROI, not reach:** Whether for products or services, focusing on conversions, qualified leads, and cost per acquisition delivers better long-term results than chasing likes or follower counts.
- **Use data-driven campaigns with continuous testing:** All three examples highlight testing, be it A/B creatives (this is a technique where one releases more than one version of an ad to check which one gives the best results), ad copy, keywords, or targeting and optimizing campaigns based on results.
- **Scalability is possible, even for medium/small players:** You don't need massive budgets. Consistent strategy, smart ad spend, and clarity on goals (brand building vs conversion) can produce meaningful growth.

Recommendations for Readers and Beginners

If you are running a small or medium business, start-up, or personal brand, here's how you can adapt these lessons:

- **Start by defining your audience and their intent.** Are they searching for a solution now, or are you trying to create interest? Choose your channel accordingly (search ads vs social + influencer).
- **Use authentic content over polished ads.** Share your story, customer testimonies, behind-the-scenes, and everyday use. People relate to real life more than glossy campaigns.

- **Test before scaling.** Run small-budget campaigns to identify what works (ads, audiences, copy), then scale the successful ones.
- **Measure results meticulously.** Track conversions, cost per lead, and ROAS, not vanity metrics.
- **Blend organic and paid strategies.** Use organic content for brand building and paid ads for reaching new or high-intent customers.
- **Be consistent and patient.** Real growth often comes from steady efforts over time, not one-off campaigns.

Limitations and What to Be Careful About

While these case studies are encouraging, it's important to acknowledge limitations and contextual factors.

- **Results vary by sector and audience.** What worked for DTC beauty or fintech may not always translate exactly for other industries.
- **Market saturation and competition matter.** As more players adopt digital marketing, cost per acquisition or competition increases.
- **Quality and execution still matter.** Good marketing can attract customers, but if product or service quality is lacking, retention will suffer.
- **Dependence on platform algorithms, and changes.** Social media platforms and ad networks change rules and algorithms. What works today may require adjustment tomorrow.

- **Data privacy and ethics.** Especially with targeted ads and re-targeting, businesses must handle user data responsibly and transparently.

Conclusion

These real-world case studies demonstrate that digital marketing, when used strategically, consistently, and ethically, can transform small start-ups and medium businesses into credible and successful brands. Whether selling products or services, the critical factors are understanding your audience, choosing the right mix of organic and paid efforts, leveraging authenticity, and optimizing for results over hype.

As you plan or refine your own digital marketing strategy, use these examples as templates – adapt to your context, test continuously, and build with clear goals.

References

1. *Economic Times*, 'How Mamaearth Built a Digital-First Brand with Facebook, Instagram and YouTube'.
2. Kirnani Technologies Blog, 'Mamaearth Case Study – ₹1000 Cr D2C Brand Growth Story'.
3. Hobo.Video Blog, 'How Mamaearth Generated Millions in Sales with Influencer Collabs'.
4. Microsoft Advertising Case Studies, 'Lenskart Strengthens Brand-Building Efforts with Search Ads'.
5. Upgrowth, 'How We Helped Lendingkart Achieve Business Growth of 20 Per Cent through Google Ads'.

Chapter 13

The Future of Digital Marketing

As digital habits continue to evolve, the world of digital marketing evolves with them. The way people discover, engage with, and purchase products has transformed dramatically in the last decade. Traditional advertisements on television, newspapers, and billboards are gradually being replaced by digital campaigns that are interactive, measurable, and highly personalized.

Today, consumers spend more time online than ever before. They browse social media, watch videos, shop on e-commerce platforms, play games, and use mobile apps throughout the day. This shift has created countless new opportunities for businesses and individuals to connect with audiences in smarter ways. However, it also means that marketers must keep up with changing technologies, platforms, and consumer preferences to stay relevant and competitive.

In this chapter, we explore the major emerging trends shaping the future of digital marketing, the upcoming career opportunities in the field, and how you can prepare for the next phase of the digital revolution.

Emerging Trends: AI, Voice, Chatbots, and Personalization

The future of digital marketing is being driven strongly by technology, automation, and the power of data. Modern marketers no longer rely only on creativity. They also depend on insights, analytics, and artificial intelligence to make smarter and faster decisions.

1. Artificial Intelligence

Artificial Intelligence is at the centre of modern digital marketing. It helps marketers collect, analyse, and use customer data efficiently. AI tools can predict user behaviour, personalize content, automate repetitive tasks, and even generate creative ideas.

For example, when you browse an e-commerce site and see 'Recommended for You', that is AI working based on your past behaviour. AI tools can also produce blog outlines, generate ad copy, and assist in customer support within seconds.

Examples of AI in Digital Marketing:

- Google Ads uses Smart Bidding to automatically adjust spending based on the best-performing ads.
- ChatGPT generates ideas, social media captions, email drafts, and replies to customer enquiries.
- Netflix and Amazon suggest shows and products based on individual preferences.

Why It Matters: AI is not replacing human marketers; it's enhancing their capabilities. Beginners can use AI tools to save time, brainstorm ideas, and improve the quality of their campaigns without requiring technical expertise.

2. Voice Search Optimization

The popularity of voice assistants like Amazon's Alexa, Apple's Siri, and Google Assistant has changed how people search for information. Instead of typing short keywords, users now speak naturally, asking complete questions.

This means marketers must optimize content to match *conversational language* rather than short search terms. Voice searches are longer, more specific, and often location-based.

Example: Instead of typing *'best bakeries'*, a person might say, *'Where can I get fresh cupcakes near me?'*

To capture such audiences, marketers need to focus on:

- Using long-tail keywords that match spoken phrases
- Optimizing Google My Business listings for local searches
- Writing content in a more conversational and question-based tone

Why It Matters: Voice search is especially relevant for local businesses, restaurants, and service providers. As smart speakers and voice-enabled devices become more common, optimizing for voice will be an essential skill for future marketers.

3. Chatbots and Marketing Automation

Chatbots are virtual assistants integrated into websites, messaging apps, or social media platforms. They can instantly answer customer questions, share product details, and even process orders – all without human involvement.

Automation tools also help manage repetitive marketing tasks such as sending follow-up emails, scheduling social media posts, or segmenting audiences based on their behaviour.

Example: A real estate website may use a chatbot that replies instantly when someone types, *'2 BHK under ₹50 lakhs'*. The chatbot can display listings, share images, and even schedule a call with an agent.

Popular Tools:

- **ManyChat** for automating WhatsApp or Facebook Messenger replies
- **HubSpot** for lead nurturing and email automation
- **Zapier** for connecting different marketing tools to work together

Why It Matters: Chatbots and automation improve efficiency and customer satisfaction. For small businesses, they offer 24/7 support without hiring a large team. For beginners, learning how to set up basic automation can be a strong professional skill.

4. Personalization

Today's customers expect more than generic advertisements. They want experiences tailored to their needs. Personalization means delivering the right message to the right person at the right time.

This is made possible through tools like **customer relationship management (CRM)** software and data analytics platforms that track customer interactions and preferences.

Examples of Personalization in Action:

- **Email marketing:** Sending customized product recommendations based on past purchases.
- **Streaming services:** Suggesting movies or music similar to what users have already enjoyed.
- **E-commerce platforms:** Showing 'Recently Viewed' or 'You May Also Like' sections on websites.

Why It Matters: Personalization makes customers feel valued and understood. It increases engagement, loyalty, and conversion rates – all critical factors in marketing success. Even small businesses can use free or affordable CRM tools to collect data and personalize communication effectively.

Other Notable Future Trends

Apart from the above, there are several upcoming trends to watch.

- **Augmented reality (AR) and virtual reality (VR):** These technologies are being used for immersive shopping experiences. For example, cosmetic brands let users 'try on' make-up virtually.
- **Video-first marketing:** Short videos on platforms like YouTube Shorts, Instagram Reels, and TikTok continue to dominate digital engagement.
- **Sustainability marketing:** Consumers now prefer eco-friendly and socially responsible brands, so marketers highlight green practices and ethical sourcing.

- **Data privacy and transparency:** With growing concerns about data protection, ethical data handling and clear consent are becoming top priorities for marketers.

Digital Careers in the Next Five Years

The digital marketing industry is growing rapidly across the world, including India. Almost every business, from start-ups to global corporations, now needs skilled digital marketers to reach online audiences.

The next five years will create exciting career paths for those who understand both creativity and technology.

In-demand roles include:

- **Social media manager:** Handles brand visibility, engagement, and community management across social platforms
- **SEO specialist:** Optimizes websites to appear higher in search results
- **Google Ads expert:** Runs paid advertising campaigns on Google
- **Content creator/copywriter:** Produces engaging blogs, videos, and ad copy
- **Data analyst:** Interprets digital performance reports and suggests improvements
- **Email marketing specialist:** Designs and manages customer communication campaigns
- **AI marketing assistant:** Uses AI tools to generate insights, automate tasks, and create content

- **Voice SEO specialist:** Optimizes content for voice search queries
- **Chatbot designer:** Creates and manages automated chatbot systems for websites or social media.
- With the growth of online certifications, freelancing platforms, and remote work, anyone – students, homemakers, or working professionals – can learn and earn in this field. Digital marketing offers flexibility, creativity, and scalability like no other profession.

Preparing for the Future

To succeed in the digital future, continuous learning is essential. The platforms, algorithms, and tools you use today may change tomorrow. What remains constant is your ability to adapt, experiment, and learn.

Here are some practical tips:

1. **Keep up with trends:** Follow digital marketing blogs, podcasts, and YouTube channels to stay updated.
2. **Experiment with tools:** Try free versions of AI, design, and analytics tools to build hands-on experience.
3. **Focus on data:** Learn how to read reports and use insights to make better marketing decisions.
4. **Develop soft skills:** Creativity, communication, and problem-solving are equally important alongside technical skills.
5. **Build a personal brand:** Showcase your skills and knowledge on platforms like LinkedIn or Instagram to attract professional opportunities.

Unlock the Complete Digital Marketing Masterclass!

Don't just read; watch, learn, and implement. We've bridged the gap between theory and reality. Your purchase includes exclusive access to one of the author's video library to ensure you master every concept in this book.

Scan Me

Dear Reader,

We hope you enjoyed reading this book and we'd love your attention for one more page, to share with you what's going on with children and books.

The number of children reading in their leisure time and for fun is in rapid decline. Young people have a lot of competition for their time, and a worryingly high number have only a few or no books at home.

If this is not a crisis already, it soon will be.

Studies have shown that reading for fun is the **single biggest predictor of a child's future success** – more than family circumstance, parents' educational background or income. It improves academic results, mental health, wealth, communication skills and ambition.

Our business works committedly to create books that are well-researched, engaging, and enduring, but here are some ways we can all raise more readers:

- Reading to children for just 10 minutes a day makes a difference
- Don't give up if children aren't regular readers – it's not just about the number of books they have or read but about encouraging interest and engagement
- Encourage them to listen to audiobooks
- Support schools and other libraries
- Give books as gifts

Thank you for reading: there's a lot more information about how to encourage children to read on our website.